What people are saying about

Slave and Sage: Remarks on the Stoic Handbook of Epictetus

Epictetus' Handbook is the best ext   count of ancient
Stoicism, and it still ranks as one   useful self-help
manuals in today's world. T   ontemporary
applications and accessib'   aiolo guides
the reader reliably th   ine Handbook to
bring out their core i   obscure by references
to ancient social cust   a philosophers. Ferraiolo
recasts many of the sayin   erience what their force meant
to ancient readers and t make seemingly counterintuitive
teachings plausible. His commentary will inspire 21st century
readers to reevaluate their assumptions on how to live a free and
contented life and question the limits of Stoic wisdom.
Lou Matz, Professor of Philosophy, University of the Pacific

This little gem of philosophical insight will help you dig down
into the best wisdom of the ancient Stoic philosopher, Epictetus,
and see how it can apply powerfully in our lives today. William
Ferraiolo has joined the lofty ranks of such recent authors as
the best-seller Ryan Holiday and the modern Stoic practitioner
William Irvine as among the most effective proponents of Stoic
thinking since the Original Big Three themselves—the Roman
lawyer and political advisor Seneca, the freed slave and famous
teacher Epictetus, and the Emperor of Rome, Marcus Aurelius.
Highly Recommended.
Tom Morris, proprietor of Tom V Morris.com and author of
such books as *True Success, If Aristotle Ran General Motors, The
Stoic Art of Living, The Oasis Within,* and *Plato's Lemonade Stand*

Other Books by this Author

Meditations on Self-Discipline and Failure: Stoic Exercise for
Mental Fitness
ISBN: 978-1-78535-587-5

A Life Worth Living: Meditations on God, Death and Stoicism
ISBN: 978-1-78904-304-4

You Die at the End: Meditations on Mortality and the Human
Condition
ISBN: 978-1-78904-393-8

God Bless the Broken Bones: Meditations over One Botched,
Bungled, and Beautiful Year
ISBN: 978-1-78904-484-3

Slave and Sage: Remarks on the Stoic Handbook of Epictetus

Slave and Sage: Remarks on the Stoic Handbook of Epictetus

William Ferraiolo

BOOKS

Winchester, UK
Washington, USA

JOHN HUNT PUBLISHING

First published by O-Books, 2021
O-Books is an imprint of John Hunt Publishing Ltd., 3 East St., Alresford,
Hampshire SO24 9EE, UK
office@jhpbooks.com
www.johnhuntpublishing.com
www.o-books.com

For distributor details and how to order please visit the 'Ordering' section on our website.

Text copyright: William Ferraiolo 2020

ISBN: 978 1 78904 671 7
978 1 78904 672 4 (ebook)
Library of Congress Control Number: 2020937437

A CIP catalogue record for this book is available from the British Library.

Design: Stuart Davies

Printed and bound by CPI Group (UK) Ltd, Croydon, CR0 4YY

We operate a distinctive and ethical publishing philosophy in
all areas of our business, from our global network of authors to
production and worldwide distribution.

Contents

Dedicated to Practicing Stoics Everywhere

The author wishes to thank everyone who reads this book and everyone who helped with the production process. Epictetus and Elizabeth Carter were particularly useful "assistants."

Introduction

The *Enchiridion* (or *Handbook*) of Epictetus is something like an abridged version of the much longer *Discourses of Epictetus*, and it was compiled by one of his students, Flavius Arrian, and thereby preserved for posterity. The *Handbook* presents the most crucial and central elements of Stoic philosophy, culled from the longer *Discourses*, and explained through the various lectures that Epictetus delivered to his students, and also by way of dialogues and other forms of interaction between the Stoic wise man and those whom he taught at his school in Nicopolis in northwestern Greece. A case can be made that Epictetus is both the wisest and most influential of the great Roman Stoic philosophers. His popularity in his own time arguably rivaled that of Plato in the years following the execution of Socrates. A lot of the content of *The Meditations of Marcus Aurelius* recapitulates, more or less, the content of Epictetus' *Discourses*. So, Epictetus was absolutely indispensable to the development and dissemination of Stoic philosophy throughout the Greco-Roman world, and also to our access to the wisdom of the Stoics and our ability to apply that wisdom to our lives in the contemporary world.

It is very difficult to argue that any of the Roman Stoics rose from humbler beginnings than did Epictetus. He was, after all, born into *slavery*. His owner, by most accounts, had him repeatedly tortured. The favored method was, evidently, twisting Epictetus' leg until one or more bones snapped. This punishment was, according to most accounts, imposed upon the budding Stoic philosopher sufficiently often that his foot, or perhaps his entire leg, pointed backward. So, Epictetus was not only born as a piece of property to be dispensed with as his owner saw fit, he was also physically crippled for the rest of his life due to repeated instances of torture. There is, however, no record of Epictetus ever complaining about these conditions of

1

his early life, and he insisted that lameness is merely a condition of the leg, and proved to be no detriment to the will or the faculty of reason. If Epictetus could live a noble, honorable, and enormously impactful life in the ancient Greco-Roman world, into which he emerged as a slave and was crippled relatively early in life, then *you* can certainly manage a noble and honorable life as well, can you not? You can, at the very least, *try* your best to do so.

The purpose of the book that you are holding is to explain the content of Epictetus' *Enchiridion* in a way that will make it accessible to contemporary readers, and there is also an attempt to demonstrate how the lessons that Epictetus offered are still applicable to *modern* circumstances and contemporary problems with which we are all presented on a fairly regular basis. The text of *this* book includes elaborations upon the text of the *Enchiridion*. Hopefully, these elaborations are consistent with the spirit of the original text.

The book you are reading is not *about* Epictetus or about his life and exploits. It *is* about his conception of Stoicism and its various applications to the human condition (and some of the longer entries in the *Enchiridion* are separated into several subsections for the purpose of more fine-grained explanation). Stoicism, the author contends, is every bit as useful and beneficial in the 21st Century as it was in the ancient Greco-Roman world. The human condition, in and of itself, has not changed a great deal over the last couple of millennia. Technology has improved and evolved by leaps and bounds, but human beings are much the same as they were in Epictetus' day. The world is still very large and powerful, humans are comparatively very small and powerless to resist the forces of nature, and every human being is born, lives for a little while (none of us knows how long we get to live), and every person who gets to live, also gets to drop dead at the end of life on this planet. Between being born and dropping dead, we try to figure out how to live these lives that we have been granted. The wisdom of Epictetus is, the author of this book contends, an enormously helpful guide to the art and practice of living well and cultivating virtue.

Some of the members of the Roman Legions are said to have carried Epictetus' *Handbook* with them when they marched on military campaigns and before they headed into battle. Presumably, they derived some form of comfort or strengthened fortitude from delving into the Stoic worldview and adopting the corresponding mindset. They could not, after all, control what they were ordered to do, where the campaign might take them, or the very real possibility of death, dismemberment, or permanent disability that might result from battle or other rigors of the military life at that stage of history. Stoic philosophy taught them, as it teaches us today, that the individual can only control his *own* will, his *own* attitude, his *own* behavior (insofar as the body cooperates), and his pursuit of virtues such as courage and self-discipline. All conditions that are external to the mind, the will, or the deliberative faculty of the individual are "indifferent" as they cannot be controlled and, thus, do not contribute to (or detract from) the character of the individual. Stoicism holds that only *you* can turn yourself into a morally decent human being, and only *you* can debase yourself through indiscipline, vice, or irrationality that degrades your character. If you focus your mind, your efforts, and your energy on becoming as wise and as virtuous a person as you are able, then you will live a better, nobler life and you can approach nearer to the Stoic ideal of *eudaimonia* (a flourishing life lived virtuously—and not mere transient "happiness"). If you are a rational person, then you will pursue the flourishing life directed by reason in a diligent effort to attain wisdom and decency. Beyond this, the rest of the external world is to be embraced with gratitude as the events therein are beyond the control of your will and not, therefore, "up to you."

The common person looks to *external* events for satisfaction, happiness, comfort, and the fulfillment of other desires. This strategy is unwise and rarely successful. Allowing your contentment to be contingent upon conditions beyond your control virtually guarantees that you will experience frustration, anger, and disappointment on a regular basis. Nonetheless, this is the way that most people live their lives. They insist that events *must* unfold thus-and-so, or they simply *cannot* be serene or at ease in the world. This is a formula for emotional disaster. Everyone that you have ever loved *is* going to die, as are *you*. Perhaps there is life *after* death, and perhaps there is not, but bodily death is pretty clearly real. If you insist that your loved ones must *not* die, must *not* suffer, and must remain with you *forever*, then you insist upon the impossible. Your misery is thereby secured. A strategy that *assures* misery is, at least to that extent, a poorly conceived strategy for managing your life, your mental states, or your emotions, and it is very difficult to imagine that such a strategy will produce lasting contentment or peace of mind.

In *this* book, you will find the wisdom of Epictetus, translated by Elizabeth Carter in the 18th Century, and you will find an attempt to update the application of the lessons Epictetus offered, so that you can utilize them to improve *your* life in the contemporary world. The author hopes that this is a useful service, and that reading this book will improve your ability to manage your psychological and emotional states. Read on and judge for yourself. The author wishes you well and thanks you for reading this book.

The Handbook (*Enchiridion*) of Epictetus

1-a. Some things are in our control and others not. Things in our control are opinion, pursuit, desire, aversion, and, in a word, whatever are our own actions. Things not in our control are body, property, reputation, command, and, in one word, whatever are not our own actions.

You have no control over *any* events other than those that you can direct by the exertion of your own will, your own faculty of deliberation and choice, with *no* assistance or mediation involving the world external to your will. This is the single most fundamental lesson from Epictetus and his elaboration of Stoic philosophy. If you fail to understand the very limited sphere over which you exert direct control, you will make no progress toward understanding the human condition, and you will suffer the lot of the common, unenlightened human being struggling, and failing, to find peace, serenity, equanimity, and a flourishing, well-lived life. You will waste a great deal of time and energy trying to change conditions that you *cannot* change, and you will fail to direct adequate time and vitality to the conditions that you *could* change if only you made the attempt with diligence and vigor. If you are uncertain whether some condition or event lies within your power, there is a simple test that you can use to distinguish the one type of condition from the other. Simply decide that the desired event will occur, or decide that the undesired event will not take place. Observe carefully. When you decided to cause the event to happen, did it? If not, that event is not within your control, at least not at present. When you decided that a particular condition would *not* come to pass, did your decision prevent the condition from arising? If not, that condition is also not up to you. Decide, for example, that you will grow another six inches taller than you are, and that you will do so *right now*. How did that go? As you see, even your *body* is not really yours to control. Age, damage, illness, and death occur whether you consent to these conditions or not. It is, therefore, unwise to obsess about conditions and events that lie beyond your control, and you ought to recognize that your time, energy, and effort is better directed at the few things that you *can* control by developing mental and moral discipline.

1-b. The things in our control are by nature free, unrestrained, unhindered; but those not in our control are weak, slavish, restrained, belonging to others. Remember, then, that if you suppose that things which are slavish by nature are also free, and that what belongs to others is your own, then you will be hindered. You will lament, you will be disturbed, and you will find fault both with gods and men. But if you suppose that only to be your own which is your own, and what belongs to others such as it really is, then no one will ever compel you or restrain you. Further, you will find fault with no one or accuse no one. You will do nothing against your will. No one will hurt you, you will have no enemies, and you will not be harmed.

You invite and ensure psychological and emotional suffering when you insist upon controlling events and affairs that are *not* yours to control. If you allow your peace of mind to depend upon events in the external world unfolding in some manner that is not "in the cards," so to speak, then your frustration, anger and despair are bound to ensue. You will find yourself blaming other people, or fate, or God, or happenstance for your misery, but you will have imposed your misery upon *yourself*. Had you remained emotionally detached from events that lie beyond the control of your own will, you would not have had any cause to lament conditions of reality as they stand or as they will unfold. You cannot be *harmed* by anyone other than yourself. You can, of course, be physically injured, killed, and tortured by other people. You can, obviously, lose money, or your job, or your house, or your family. These events do not, however, constitute *harm* to your *will*, or to your *character*. None of those events can *degrade* you or cause you to become a *morally* diminished being. You can abase *yourself* through immoral or irrational conduct, but no one else can *force* you to do so. If you make an immoral person of yourself, therefore, you have only *yourself* to blame. Do not forget that you have the capacity to *ennoble* yourself as well. If you devote yourself to the project of making yourself a better and wiser person, you are not going to have the inclination to regard other persons as enemies, as they cannot do you any real harm, and you will live untroubled by the words and deeds of persons other than yourself.

1-c. Aiming therefore at such great things, remember that you must not allow yourself to be carried, even with a slight tendency, towards the attainment of lesser things. Instead, you must entirely quit some things and for the present postpone the rest. But if you would both have these great things, along with power and riches, then you will not gain even the latter, because you aim at the former too: but you will absolutely fail of the former, by which alone happiness and freedom are achieved.

If you wish to improve your character, to attain greater wisdom than you possess right now, and to become a more virtuous person, then you must learn to disregard the impulse to pursue base attainments such as wealth, power, or fame. Allowing your contentment to attach to and depend upon such conditions is both unwise and unhealthy. Wealth, power, and fame will never make you a *morally* better person or a wiser individual than you are without them. The pursuit of "lesser things," such as material gain, is also very likely to lead you into immoral behavior and compromises of your decency. Thieves, for example, desire money and property to which they have neither any moral nor legal right. If you aim to become an honorable person, then you cannot also divert much of your time and effort to becoming rich and powerful. All of the energy you spend on the latter pursuits is energy that you cannot direct at self-improvement and enhancing your understanding of the world, your place in it, and the proper way to go about becoming a wiser and more virtuous human being. You will simply enslave yourself to the mechanisms of becoming wealthy, powerful, and famous. There is nothing honorable about *that*. You will deprive yourself of the freedom that comes only from self-rectification and moral self-discipline. Even if you gain material advantages or benefits, then you must realize that you *will* be stripped of them either during this life or at its end. You cannot, as the saying goes, "take it with you." Where is the wisdom in pursuing wealth at the expense of virtue? Even if you manage to acquire the wealth, how will you use your money if you have not acquired wisdom and virtue? A vicious scoundrel does not make the world a better place and, in fact, does not even make himself a better person. His is a lowly, though wealthy, existence.

1-d. Work, therefore to be able to say to every harsh appearance, "You are but an appearance, and not absolutely the thing you appear to be." And then examine it by those rules which you have, and first, and chiefly, by this: whether it concerns the things which are in our own control, or those which are not; and, if it concerns anything not in our control, be prepared to say that it is nothing to you.

With assiduous practice and the diligent and gradual development and enhancement of your mental discipline, you can learn to distinguish between mere appearances and objective reality, and you can also develop the ability to resist the impulse to regard events as catastrophic or terrible just because most people regard them as awful, or just because the occurrence involves damage to a person, place, or thing with which you are associated or to which you have some misguided emotional attachment. If, for example, you lose your job, the initial temptation may be to react with anger, indignation, or despair, but, upon carefully reasoned analysis, you will realize that your job is not *yours* to *control*, and your superiors at work have the ability to terminate your employment any time that they decide that you are no longer welcome as an employee. The dispensation of the terms of your employment is *not* within your control, and even the most diligent employee can be fired with or without just cause. The company can go bankrupt. Corrupt management can hollow it out and destroy all the jobs dependent upon it. If you realize that you have become ill, you need not add emotional disturbance about your ailment to the viral or bacterial infection and physiological consequences thereof. Illness and injury are not pleasant, but nothing about either type of condition *compels* you to become despondent about what is happening to your body. The same may be said of old age, alterations to your appearance, and other inevitable frailties of human embodiment. Your *attitude* about the condition of your body is entirely within your control, though the actual condition of it is not. The mind is yours to control, but not the body. Let the appearances associated with your body, your surrounding environment, and all other conditions that lie beyond your control serve as data and information about the world, but do not allow such appearances to trouble you or impair your equanimity.

2. Remember that following desire promises the attainment of that of which you are desirous; and aversion promises the avoiding that to which you are averse. However, he who fails to obtain the object of his desire is disappointed, and he who incurs the object of his aversion wretched. If, then, you confine your aversion to those objects only which are contrary to the natural use of your faculties, which you have in your own control, you will never incur anything to which you are averse. But if you are averse to sickness, or death, or poverty, you will be wretched. Remove aversion, then, from all things that are not in our control, and transfer it to things contrary to the nature of what is in our control. But, for the present, totally suppress desire: for, if you desire any of the things which are not in your own control, you must necessarily be disappointed; and of those which are, and which it would be laudable to desire, nothing is yet in your possession. Use only the appropriate actions of pursuit and avoidance; and even these lightly, and with gentleness and reservation.

If you choose to pursue a desire, then you must be prepared for the possibility that you will fail to attain what you desire, or for the possibility that you *will* attain what you desire, and then you will find that you are *disappointed* by the experience. If you form aversions to certain kinds of experiences, then you may very well incur the experience to which you are averse, and then you will be dissatisfied or frustrated because of your aversion. If you are averse to death, then you *will* incur *that* aversion. You can insulate yourself from disappointment and dissatisfaction only by restricting your desires and aversions to conditions that you can bring into being through the exertion of your will, and events that you can prevent simply by deciding that the events will not occur. Clearly the only events and conditions that you can control are those that are subject to no power other than your will and your capacity to make decisions. If you are averse to lying, do not lie. In this way, you can only incur your aversion if you fail to discipline yourself to avoid telling lies. There is no one else to blame if you suffer from such a failure. *Who* has the power to turn you into a liar? When you first begin to practice Stoicism, perhaps it is best to relinquish *all* desire and aversion, as best you are able, otherwise you are bound to be frustrated in one fashion or another. Gradually, you will find that you can safely attune your desires and aversions in rational and virtuous fashion, but this will take assiduous practice and effort.

3. With regard to whatever objects give you delight, are useful, or are deeply loved, remember to tell yourself of what general nature they are, beginning from the most insignificant things. If, for example, you are fond of a specific ceramic cup, remind yourself that it is only ceramic cups in general of which you are fond. Then, if it breaks, you will not be disturbed. If you kiss your child, or your wife, say that you only kiss things which are human, and thus you will not be disturbed if either of them dies.

Remember that when it comes to all the things to which you allow yourself to become emotionally attached, that external objects, conditions, and even human beings, are all fragile, ephemeral, and subject to change and destruction. Nothing in the material world lasts *forever*. If you have some favorite possessions, then you should understand that you cannot and will not possess them forever. Physical objects can be lost, broken, or stolen, and you will be separated from them either before you die or *when* you die. This lesson also applies to the people whom you love and care for the most. Your spouse, your siblings, your parents, and your children, no matter how dearly you love them, are only mortals, just as *you* are only a mortal, and all persons are subject to illness, injury, imprisonment, mistreatment and death. Remind yourself as often as is necessary that loving another human being, while it is a noble and healthy element of a well-lived life, does not prevent the eventuality that your beloved will be separated from you, will suffer in various ways, and will, inevitably, go "the way of all flesh," and end up as dead as all other people who have lived and died. There is nothing you can do about that fact that all human beings are both frail and mortal. Insisting that your loved ones must not suffer and die guarantees that you will despair. So, do not insist upon the impossible if you wish to avoid needless suffering. You really should not *insist* upon anything at all apart from your own mental states and the proper governance of your own behavior. Perhaps it is advisable to consider everything that you own, every condition of your life, and every facet of your circumstances, and take a moment to remind yourself that "this too shall pass away." Everything does, after all.

4. When you are going about any action, remind yourself what nature the action is. If you are going to bathe, picture to yourself the things which usually happen in the bath: some people splash the water, some push, some use abusive language, and others steal. Thus you will more safely go about this action if you say to yourself, "I will now go bathe, and keep my own mind in a state conformable to nature." And in the same manner with regard to every other action. For thus, if any hindrance arises in bathing, you will have it ready to say, "It was not only to bathe that I desired, but to keep my mind in a state conformable to nature; and I will not keep it if I am bothered at things that happen."

Maintain a "reserve clause" when you set about any endeavor that you choose to undertake. Recognize that the external world may not permit you to do what you intend to do, and be aware that events may turn out differently than you had anticipated, or in a way that proves to be incompatible with your plans coming to fruition. If, for example, you plan to go to the movies, remind yourself that your car could break down, the tickets could be sold out, the projection equipment could malfunction, and many other events could forestall your intention to see the movie you have chosen. Even if you successfully make it into the theater, and there are not any technological malfunctions, there may be people who talk loudly during the film, or someone may throw popcorn, or you may find yourself seated next to someone suffering a coughing fit. Tell yourself that you will see the movie, *provided* that circumstances permit you to do so. Admonish yourself to remain patient if things do not quite go according to plan, and resist the urge to become angry or frustrated at other moviegoers who behave in a manner that is inconsistent with your goals. Keep your cool even if things go "awry" in the sense that events deviate from your expectations.

Also, learn to manage your expectations in a more rationally governed fashion. What gives you the right to expect *anything* to transpire as you choose, apart from your own thoughts and conduct? Whatever you aim to do, you should aim to do it *and* to maintain your equanimity and your dignity. Do not trade away your peace of mind for the sake of getting out and about.

5. Men are disturbed, not by things, but by the principles and notions which they form concerning things. Death, for instance, is not terrible, else it would have appeared so to Socrates. But the terror consists in our notion of death that it is terrible. When therefore we are hindered, or disturbed, or grieved, let us never attribute it to others, but to ourselves; that is, to our own principles. An uninstructed person will lay the fault of his own bad condition upon others. Someone just starting instruction will lay the fault on himself. Some who is perfectly instructed will place blame neither on others nor on himself.

Events unfolding as they do cannot trouble you so long as you do not judge events to be disturbing or terrible, and so long as you do not tether your contentment to any particular condition of the external world. The world as it is will only bother you if you insist that the world *must be* other than it is and, of course, the world *cannot* be other than it is. Death and mortality strike most people as horrible and terrifying, but that is only because most people desire more life than is allotted to them as mere mortal human beings. The only way to avoid dying, at least up to this point in the development of medical science, is to avoid being born in the first place. Neither your birth nor that fact that you were born mortal is up to you or under your control. You and everyone you love *will* die sooner or later, and you do not know how much time anyone has. Socrates was far more averse to *degrading* himself through cowardice, criminality, or impiety than he was to his own death. He could have avoided drinking the hemlock, but he chose to die rather than debase himself. Once you understand that death is the natural culmination of life, and that you cannot simply *decide* that you will never die, this will leave you free to focus your energy on becoming as wise and as virtuous as you are able in the time that you have. Blame neither yourself nor anyone else for any *inevitability*. The inevitable is notoriously difficult to avoid. Is it not foolish to insist upon avoiding an event that is unavoidable? Do not blame the world, do not blame other persons, and do not blame yourself when events unfold as they do. What good, after all, does blame and consternation do for anyone?

6. Don't be prideful with any excellence that is not your own. If a horse should be prideful and say, "I am handsome," it would be supportable. But when you are prideful, and say, "I have a handsome horse," know that you are proud of what is, in fact, only the good of the horse. What, then, is your own? Only your reaction to the appearances of things. Thus, when you behave conformably to nature in reaction to how things appear, you will be proud with reason; for you will take pride in some good of your own.

You have no business taking pride in your wealth, your appearance, your possessions, or any power or position that you may have attained within your career or your social circle. Anything that you attain, other than wisdom and virtue, must be the result, at least in part, of happenstance, and these attainments depend upon collaboration or cooperation involving elements of the world over which you have no control whatsoever. If you are born into a wealthy family, that is just the "luck of the draw." If you attain wealth because of ingenuity and hard work, then you ought to recognize that you have been afforded both the intellectual capacity and the circumstances to *allow* you to become wealthy. Had you been born in an impoverished nation, or had you been born with a cognitive defect or a significant physiological disability, you would probably not have done so well in terms of material gain. Physically attractive people are born with either genetic endowments toward beauty, or they are provided with circumstances and opportunities that enable them to *become* attractive. Physical beauty can be stripped away from you at any moment, and no one remains beautiful forever. You may be proud of yourself when you resist the temptation to do something discreditable so as to advance your material well-being, or when you apply your best consistent efforts to developing wisdom and self-discipline. There is nothing wrong with noticing that you have made a bit of progress. As for conditions *external* to your will, you ought to recognize that all such things are matters of dumb luck. It is one thing to take pride in behaving according to reason even when you encounter the temptation to do otherwise, but you should never take pride in accidents of fate or circumstances that are determined by conditions of the external world.

7. Consider when, on a voyage, your ship is anchored; if you go on shore to get water you may along the way amuse yourself with picking up a shellfish, or an onion. However, your thoughts and continual attention ought to be bent towards the ship, waiting for the captain to call on board; you must then immediately leave all these things, otherwise you will be thrown into the ship, bound neck and feet like a sheep. So it is with life. If, instead of an onion or a shellfish, you are given a wife or child, that is fine. But if the captain calls, you must run to the ship, leaving them, and regarding none of them. But if you are old, never go far from the ship: lest, when you are called, you should be unable to come in time.

All of your possessions, all of your powers to control the material world, and all of your relations, including your immediate family, are "yours" only in the sense that you get to be with them and take care of them as best you are able, until all of those things are "reclaimed" by nature. Treat all of the persons and "furniture" of your life in the same way that you might treat a rental car, or in the manner that you would take care of a child that you are babysitting. You are responsible for the persons and possessions in your care for the time being, but you must "hold" all such things loosely, knowing that nothing is inseparable from you except for your own will and the direction of your mental energies. When "the captain calls," and your life ends, you ought to be psychologically and emotionally prepared to go where you have no choice but to go, and you ought to realize that no amount of complaining, bargaining, or pleading will enable you to remain one more moment among the people you love. Prepare yourself, and help them prepare, for the inevitable end of your time together on this planet. Everything in the material world will be taken from you, but nothing prevents you from enjoying what you have now and doing your very best to govern it wisely.

Take care of the things that you can, and do not allow yourself to be troubled by those things that you cannot control. Getting upset about the things that you cannot control has never done anyone any good. One of the conditions over which you have no control is the fact that you are mortal, you will die someday, and you have no idea when that day will come. Hopefully, you will be engaged in some virtuous behavior when "the captain calls."

8. Don't demand that things happen as you wish, but wish that they happen as they do happen, and you will go on well.

Insisting that events *must* occur in the way that you *want* them to occur, or demanding that the world *must* be the way that you desire it to be, irrespective of natural causes and consequences, is irrational and is also guaranteed to result in dissatisfaction for you. The world, as it turns out, does not *need* your permission for anything. If you decide that you *cannot* be content unless events transpire in some way that you cannot *cause* them to transpire, then you are going to be miserable when the necessary conditions for your contentment do not come to pass. When you allow your peace of mind to depend upon other persons behaving as you would have them behave, or circumstances unfolding as you think that they *ought* to unfold, then you are not going to allow yourself to be at peace very often or for very long. You are better off approaching your relationship with reality from the opposite perspective. Observe the facts as they stand, do your best to understand causes and effects that are independent of your decisions, and learn to make your desires *conform* to the way of nature and the world as it stands and as events therein transpire. If it is raining, do not insist upon sunshine, but rather learn how to appreciate the rain and accomplish what you can while the rain is falling. If your nation goes to war, you are better off learning how you can accommodate the facts as they stand, than you would be if you were to insist that the war *must* end when and how you say it must end. You do not control the military or the foreign policy of your nation's current administration. If you did, the nation would not be engaged in a war of which you disapprove. You can, however, control your *attitude* about the things that you *cannot* control, and you can learn to retain your serenity come what may in the external world. Whatever the world may throw at you, it is always within your power to retain your fortitude and your resolve. You do not *have* to allow your heart to be troubled. Develop the practice of observing events as they transpire and attuning your desires to match the world as it is, rather than petulantly insisting that the world *must* be otherwise.

9. Sickness is a hindrance to the body, but not to your ability to choose, unless that is your choice. Lameness is a hindrance to the leg, but not to your ability to choose. Say this to yourself with regard to everything that happens, then you will see such obstacles as hindrances to something else, but not to yourself.

Everyone gets sick because no one has the power simply to *decide* to be invulnerable to viruses, bacteria, and congenital defects. Epictetus, arguably the greatest Stoic philosopher ever to have lived, was born a slave and, according to canonical accounts, was disabled because his owner repeatedly had him tortured. The method of torture involved twisting his leg until it broke. Evidently, his owner had this done to the same leg many times over. Of course, the leg never healed properly. Despite being born a slave to a man who had him permanently crippled, Epictetus eventually established a school at Nicopolis and became one of the most influential philosophers in the Greco-Roman world. Thus, Epictetus demonstrated, through the example of his own life and experiences, that physical disability and disadvantageous circumstances are not a justification for despair or resignation to living an unfulfilling life. You *can* decide that you will bear any circumstance that may be thrust upon you with grace, resolve, and rational determination. No ailment or injury can prevent you from living an admirable life in conformity with nature, and within the physical limitations you may encounter. Everyone, after all, faces *some* form of limitation or other. No one is free to cast off the laws of nature or the boundaries inherent to the human condition. There are people, nonetheless, that have lived lives worthy of emulation. You can make yourself wiser and more virtuous even if your body falters and even if circumstances are far less than comfortable. If a crippled slave can live a life worth living, then surely *you* can do so as well. Do you claim to have had a more difficult life than Epictetus? Do you have a better excuse for your failures than slavery and permanent disability? Do not "cripple" yourself with frustration and resentment when sickness, injuries, or other challenges befall you. The human body is susceptible to such things. Would you prefer to *not have* a body?

10. With every accident, ask yourself what abilities you have for making a proper use of it. If you see an attractive person, you will find that self-restraint is the ability you have against your desire. If you are in pain, you will find fortitude. If you hear unpleasant language, you will find patience. And thus habituated, the appearances of things will not hurry you away along with them.

Happenstance will hurl all sorts of circumstances, events, and various people into your path. You cannot control the things that chance or nature determines that you will encounter. You *can*, however, control what you *do with*, and what you do *about*, the things that the world sets in store for you. If you are married, and you have disciplined yourself to avoid adultery no matter what form of temptation you encounter, then you should have no fear of falling into any temptation. Indeed, if you *feel* temptation, then you have more self-disciplining to do. If you are beset by some illness or injury, and if you have developed your ability to endure any kind of pain and any kind of disability with reason and serenity, then you should have no fear of any physical condition that may befall you. If you encounter any form of language, hand gestures, or facial expressions, and if you recognize that other people have the ability to say, to do, and to look as they please, then you ought to remain serene irrespective of the way that anyone behaves toward you or toward anyone else. Control your *own* behavior, your *own* utterances, and your *own* facial expressions. All of that is up to *you*. What other people may do is not yours to control, and it is irrational for you to insist that others *must* do *only* those things that you decide they are permitted to do. Do not allow your emotional states to be determined by persons or conditions that you have no power to control. Governing *your own* conduct must be sufficient to maintain your peace of mind, or you must give up on serenity, equanimity, and living a life in accordance with reason and in pursuit of decency. Avoid the common tendencies to regard some events as inherently "terrible" or irretrievably "catastrophic." Every occurrence can be used for rational purposes and can serve as an opportunity for self-improvement.

11. Never say of anything, "I have lost it"; but, "I have returned it." Is your child dead? It is returned. Is your wife dead? She is returned. Is your estate taken away? Well, and is not that likewise returned? "But he who took it away is a bad man." What difference is it to you who the giver assigns to take it back? While he gives it to you to possess, take care of it; but don't view it as your own, just as travelers view a hotel.

You cannot lose anything that was never really in your possession to begin with. It is one thing to love your children, and it is noble and admirable to do everything in your power to protect them and care for them. From this, it does not follow that you have the power to prevent every terrible event that can befall your children. Your kids can become ill, they can be injured, and they can (and eventually *will*) die. The same is true of your spouse. Love your spouse the best that you can for as long as you can, and do everything in your power to protect and to serve your spouse. You must, however, acknowledge that you do not have the capacity to ensure that your spouse will not suffer. Your spouse is fragile and mortal, as is the case with all of humanity. It is also reasonable to protect your property and maintain it as best you can, but powerful individuals and agencies can take your property away from you with or without legitimate justification. Suppose that corrupt persons who manage to make it appear that you have defaulted on your home loan, though you have, in fact, made every payment on time, deprive you of your home. This is an injustice, but it is not impossible, and you may not have the power to regain ownership of your home. If this is how events transpire, then you do yourself no favors by adding indignation and enervation to your circumstances. Think of your home as a rental property that can be reclaimed from you at the owner's whim. If this kind of event comes to pass, let go of the property that you used to control with equanimity and devote your energies to something more important than mere property. Look at your home and recognize that someone else will live in it after you die (either that or it will be bulldozed to make way for something else). Even if you own your home, you are really only "renting" it. You do *not* get to keep it forever. The things that you can buy are simply *not* very important. Wisdom and virtue *cannot* be purchased. They are *not* for sale.

12-a. If you want to improve, reject such reasonings as these: "If I neglect my affairs, I'll have no income; if I don't correct my servant, he will be bad." For it is better to die with hunger, exempt from grief and fear, than to live in affluence with perturbation; and it is better your servant should be bad, than you unhappy.

You should not be willing to trade your peace of mind for money, power, fame, or for other material advantages. All of the money in the world cannot purchase serenity, decency, or wisdom. If you value the cardinal virtues of wisdom, courage, temperance, and justice, then those will be your overarching concerns, and you will have little excess time or energy to devote to the pursuit of wealth or those things that money can buy. You are better off living (and *dying*) in poverty than living in a mansion and piloting a yacht while constantly vexed with fear, anger, and frustration. It is better to be poor and virtuous than to be wealthy and vicious, if those are the only alternatives that you find on offer. If you have employees or subordinates at work, you should not obsess about overseeing their performance on the job or micromanaging them. Perhaps your subordinates will perform poorly if you do not watch them like a hawk, but that is preferable to driving yourself to distraction with obsessive surveillance of their every act and utterance. You are in a better condition if you are calm and in possession of your faculties than if you are constantly upset by mistakes that your coworkers might make. Maintain your serenity and dignity no matter what your financial circumstances might be, and irrespective of what other people might be doing. It is not your place to govern the material world, nor is it up to you to determine how other people engage in their careers. Your job is to do the best that you can with every obligation with which you are presented and to stay calm, reasonable, and honorable irrespective of any circumstance you may encounter. Poverty can befall anyone. Illness befalls nearly everyone. Death takes *everyone*. The world *will* have its way, and you ought not try to govern the world. You *will* fail. Governing *yourself* and *your* character is something that you can manage if you devote yourself to the project in earnest. So, get to work on governing your mind and your conduct.

12-b. Begin therefore from little things. Is a little oil spilt? A little wine stolen? Say to yourself, "This is the price paid for equanimity, for tranquility, and nothing is to be had for nothing." When you call your servant, it is possible that he may not come; or, if he does, he may not do what you want. But he is by no means of such importance that it should be in his power to give you any disturbance.

It is a good idea to begin by learning to maintain your tranquility when *little* inconveniences pop up, and to make gradual progress toward retaining your peacefulness when greater challenges arise. If you spill the coffee or burn the toast as you are preparing your breakfast in the morning, then use the event as an opportunity to remind yourself that things like this are bound to happen, and simply exert the effort to remain calm when these circumstances arise, recognizing that this is just the price of maintaining your equanimity. Every event provides you an opportunity to practice mental discipline and improve your self-control. If your children disobey you or misbehave, then you have a chance to develop your patience and to engage in wise, rational communication with people to whom you ought to be an admirable role model. Your coworkers may not do their jobs properly, or they may create difficulties that require extra and unnecessary work on your part. If this comes to pass, losing your head or becoming angry will do you no good, and it will not get the work done any faster or better. Your business is to maintain your dignity and your rational self-control irrespective of events and persons that you *cannot* control. The things that are not within your power, are not important enough for you to sacrifice your composure. Nothing is more important than your attainment of virtue, and you are not particularly likely to attain virtue if you are constantly getting upset about the way that events turn out. Emotional duress is not good for the mind or the body, and it does not contribute to your self-improvement. Never cede your power to guide your mind and your attitudes to other persons or to events that lie beyond your control. Doing so is a recipe for emotional disaster.

13. If you want to improve, be content to be thought foolish and stupid with regard to external things. Don't wish to be thought to know anything; and even if you appear to be somebody important to others, distrust yourself. For, it is difficult to both keep your faculty of choice in a state conformable to nature, and at the same time acquire external things. But while you are careful about the one, you must of necessity neglect the other.

There is no great advantage in being perceived to be pragmatic or knowledgeable, and there may be some benefit in being regarded as ignorant or foolish when it comes to the attainment of material wealth and power. Though most people regard material gain as very important and as indicative of intelligence or success, the accumulation of money and possessions should not be particularly important to *you*. Your overarching goals should be the attainment of wisdom, virtue, and the improvement of your character. Having a lot of money or a fancy house will not make you more virtuous or wiser. Do your peers think that you know nothing about managing your finances? So be it. Perhaps many of them know nothing about managing their behavior and thought patterns. Who is in the more admirable condition, a person who lives in a mansion but cares nothing for self-mastery and righteousness, or a homeless person who is rational, honest, decent, and at peace with all circumstances that may arise? You cannot, as the old expression goes, "serve two masters." It is *possible* to be both wealthy and virtuous, but the acquisition of material goods often occurs at the expense of integrity, or to the detriment of character development. If you work sixteen hours a day trying to make money and amass power, then you leave yourself precious little time and energy to devote to accumulating wisdom about the human condition and the flourishing life. Do not trade away the hours of your life for mere money or position. Your life and your character are worth more than any amount of money, power, or fame for which you might sacrifice them. It is one thing to sacrifice your life for your family, your nation, or innocents in your care, but it is quite something else for you to sacrifice your life or your decency for the mere "stuff" of the material world.

14. If you wish your children, and your wife, and your friends to live for ever, you are stupid; for you wish to be in control of things which you cannot, you wish for things that belong to others to be your own. So likewise, if you wish your servant to be without fault, you are a fool; for you wish vice not to be vice, but something else. But, if you wish to have your desires undisappointed, this is in your own control. Exercise, therefore, what is in your control. He is the master of every other person who is able to confer or remove whatever that person wishes either to have or to avoid. Whoever, then, would be free, let him wish nothing, let him decline nothing, which depends on others else he must necessarily be a slave.

Insisting that you *cannot* be at peace or that you will be miserable if your loved ones ever die or if they suffer from injuries or illness, is an attitude that guarantees you will never have a moment of ease or serenity, and all of your discontent will not prevent your loved ones from suffering and dying. All of the events and conditions that you cannot control are impervious to your concerns and your efforts. If you want your children or your coworkers to behave perfectly at *all* times, then you insist upon a circumstance that can never occur, and that is nothing short of a perfect recipe for frustration, dissatisfaction, and despair. If you want to make sure that your desires are never unfulfilled, then you *must* restrict your desires to conditions that are subject to *your* control. If you want to avoid adultery, then you simply decline to engage in that behavior and you have nothing else to fear regarding the matter. Refusing to become an adulterer is *entirely* up to you. If you desire things that other persons control, then you are voluntarily enslaving yourself to those persons and handing them power to determine your mental states. Do not allow your peace of mind or your behavior to be determined by other persons, conditions of the world, or irrational desires.

Doing so will never lead you to wisdom, virtue, or the experience of equanimity. Do not allow other persons or circumstances to dictate your frame of mind. The capacity to decide *that* belongs entirely to *you*. When you allow yourself to desire something or some condition that is controlled by someone or something other than yourself, you thereby enslave yourself to the mechanisms of control.

15. Remember that you must behave in life as at a dinner party. Is anything brought around to you? Put out your hand and take your share with moderation. Does it pass by you? Don't stop it. Is it not yet come? Don't stretch your desire towards it, but wait till it reaches you. Do this with regard to children, to a wife, to public posts, to riches, and you will eventually be a worthy partner of the feasts of the gods. And if you don't even take the things which are set before you, but are able even to reject them, then you will not only be a partner at the feasts of the gods, but also of their empire. For, by doing this, Diogenes, Heraclitus and others like them, deservedly became, and were called, divine.

Learn to accept life and its various experiences and opportunities as they present themselves to you, and try not to extend your desires toward conditions, events, and material items that you may not be able to obtain. If an opportunity passes by and you are unable to avail yourself of its benefits, then you have not really lost anything significant. You cannot, after all, "lose" what you never *possessed* in the first place. You may hope to get married and start a family someday, but you should do so with the "reserve clause" in mind, and aim for these things *if* God or Fate allows for the conditions at which you aim to happen. Perhaps you will never find a suitable spouse, or maybe you will get married but find that you are unable to procreate. No matter what eventualities unfold, you always have it within your power to maintain your dignity and your equanimity, irrespective of any circumstances that may arise. Ideally, you may develop such fortitude and strength of mental discipline that you will have neither need nor desire for anything that is not within the direct control of your will. Diogenes was, according to legend (probably apocryphal), sunbathing one day when Alexander the Great visited him and offered the old Cynic philosopher anything that he cared to name. Diogenes asked only that Alexander move aside and stop blocking his sunlight. Alexander respected his independence and said that if he were not Alexander, he would wish to be Diogenes. The great conqueror understood that he had encountered a man whom he could never conquer. Alexander could, of course, *kill* Diogenes, but that would not constitute a conquest of his indomitable *soul*. Everyone is going to die. *You* are going to die. Between now and then, do you intend to make yourself into the wisest and most virtuous person you are able? You should, perhaps, hope so.

16. When you see anyone weeping in grief because his son has gone abroad, or is dead, or because he has suffered in his affairs, be careful that the appearance may not misdirect you. Instead, distinguish within your own mind, and be prepared to say, "It's not the accident that distresses this person, because it doesn't distress another person; it is the judgment which he makes about it." As far as words go, however, don't reduce yourself to his level, and certainly do not moan with him. Do not moan inwardly either.

Many of your friends, coworkers, and neighbors are going to experience illness and death within their immediate families. Eventually, *all* of them will. They are also going to encounter all sorts of difficulties involving finances, disappointments involving children and their circumstances, and many other events that will cause them distress and bring them to tears. When this happens, do not allow yourself to be drawn into their state of discontent or frustration. Recognize that the events themselves are not *intrinsically* terrible. All of the people who do *not* know your friends, coworkers, neighbors, or your family are going about their lives unmoved by the sorrows that people of your acquaintance, but not *theirs*, experience. It may not be appropriate or helpful to tell people that their supposed "problems" are not really worth the moaning and groaning, but do not join them in their despair either, as that does them no good, and is also a departure from rationality. Do not expect everyone to embrace your understanding of what is most important, especially when they are in the grip of grief or anguish, but cling to the dictates of reason in all things as they appear to you. You need not indulge in grieving merely because a friend of yours experiences grief. Be prepared to help as best you can, if indeed you can offer any assistance at all, but do not allow your mind or your mood to become caught up in the emotional turmoil that you witness. Emotional tumult is not good for you and it does not lead to wise decisions or admirable behavior. Your mind is most effective as a tool when you are calm and rational. If you are "groaning" either outwardly or inwardly, your faculty of reason is probably not functioning at full capacity, and you are likely to be distracted from your proper purposes by grief and mourning.

17. Remember that you are an actor in a drama, of such a kind as the author pleases to make it. If short, of a short one; if long, of a long one. If it is his pleasure you should act a poor man, a cripple, a governor, or a private person, see that you act it naturally. For this is your business, to act well the character assigned you; to choose it is another's.

Neither you nor anyone else gets to choose the time, place, or conditions into which any of us is born, nor do any of us get to choose the laws of nature or the course of history prior to our births. You may be born into wealth, or into poverty, or into any other material conditions at all. You may be born male, you may be born female, or you may be born with indeterminate sex. As for race, ethnicity, or the nation into which you are born, none of that is up to you either. None of the fundamental features of your physical person, determined by genetics and happenstance, is subject to your choice or your desire. Each of us just "shows up" as a unique bit of humanity on this planet that we did not create, in a cosmos over which we have no control, and subject to laws of nature that take no notice of us or our interests. If you rise to a position of political power, then conduct yourself as a virtuous and rational agent engaged in the project of proper governance. If you find that you are impoverished, and that your best efforts cannot alter that circumstance, then you are obligated to endure your poverty with equanimity and live the life of a rational and honorable street dweller. Diogenes managed as much, and what one person can do another ought to be able to accomplish as well. A husband and father should play that role to the best of his ability, and a wife and mother should do her best within that set of responsibilities. Doing the best that you can, irrespective of circumstances, is the noblest attainment that anyone can manage. You do not *create* yourself, but you can learn to govern your behavior in wise fashion. Indeed, the appropriate governance of your mind and your behavior is really the best that you (or anyone else) will ever manage. The governance of others and of the world at large is not granted to you. Use your energies and your efforts to play the role you have been assigned to the best of your abilities. You do not know how long you get to be "on stage" or what future turns the production may take.

18. When a raven happens to croak unluckily, don't allow the appearance hurry you away with it, but immediately make the distinction to yourself, and say, "None of these things are foretold to me; but either to my paltry body, or property, or reputation, or children, or wife. But to me all omens are lucky, if I will. For whichever of these things happens, it is in my control to derive advantage from it."

Many events occur that various people will tell you constitute evil omens, or that some may describe as harbingers of doom, or unlucky signs of allegedly terrible things to come. Perhaps a black cat will cross your path. Maybe you will inadvertently break a mirror. The number thirteen may crop up somewhere. All fear attaching to any of this kind of thing is superstitious nonsense, of course, but even if it were not, and even if breaking a mirror really did cause you to incur seven years of bad luck, that would not prevent you from learning how to manage your affairs amid the "unlucky" times, or from maintaining rational control of your mind and your actions so as to turn all events into opportunities to learn something, or to endure some unpleasantness with a noble spirit. Do not allow your mind to succumb to despair because of some allegedly ill tidings, but rather treat all circumstances as opportunities to bear pain and suffering with grace, or to forbear any impulse or temptation to debase yourself through weakness, indiscipline, or irrationality. If your body falls ill or is damaged by injury, then you have the opportunity to respond with courage and fortitude. Should you lose some property or see it irreparably damaged, you have the ability to remind yourself that mere property has nothing to do with your moral purpose and your rational self-discipline. Those who speak ill of you provide you with a valuable occasion to remain untroubled by their irrelevant recriminations. The words that other persons speak are not yours to control, and they determine nothing about your character. Why concern yourself with noises that other people make with their faces? There can be no "harbingers of doom" for you, so long as you maintain rational governance of your mind and conduct yourself in virtuous fashion.

19. You may be unconquerable, if you enter into no combat in which it is not in your own control to conquer. When, therefore, you see anyone eminent in honors, or power, or in high esteem on any other account, take heed not to be hurried away with the appearance, and to pronounce him happy; for, if the essence of good consists in things in our own control, there will be no room for envy or emulation. But, for your part, don't wish to be a general, or a senator, or a consul, but to be free; and the only way to this is a contempt of things not in our own control.

You cannot be defeated if you compete *only* in arenas that are determined by the control of *your* will or your faculty of deliberation and choice. Who can defeat you in the competition to direct your thoughts and actions in rational and responsible fashion? In any other sort of competition, remember that winning the contest is not a proper goal, but rather doing your best and maintaining your dignity should be your aim. Can anyone *force* you to fail in either respect? As for people who have won many trophies, awards, accolades, and who have secured positions of prominence and power, you should not assume that those are indications of real success. Consider all of the headaches that go along with occupying a political position, and all of the unwanted scrutiny that comes with fame or notoriety. If you want to be free from all of the needless annoyances and nuisances that the rich, famous, and powerful have to put up with, and if your primary goal is to live a simple life that conforms to reason and modesty, then you have no good reason to envy those people whose fame, fortune, and power make it *more* difficult to live the type of life that you pursue. If you have no interest in wealth, then you should not regard those who are wealthier than you as more successful than you. They merely have more money than you. The famous also have more of something for which you simply have no use or interest. Surely, this is not a cause for envy or frustration. The fact that someone else possesses something that you do *not* want is hardly a "problem" or a tragedy. All of the things that you do *not* want can be distributed in any manner at all without causing you the slightest discomfort of dissatisfaction. What, after all, do you care for the things that you do not want? You can free yourself of all needless concern and despair if you simply relinquish your uneasiness about matters that lie beyond your control.

20. Remember, that not he who gives ill language or a blow insults, but the principle which represents these things as insulting. When, therefore, anyone provokes you, be assured that it is your own opinion which provokes you. Try, therefore, in the first place, not to be hurried away with the appearance. For if you once gain time and respite, you will more easily command yourself.

No one has the ability to insult or offend you without your complicity, and if you ever feel insulted or offended, you ought to understand that you have caused *yourself* to experience events in this way, *you* have caused your own psychological and emotional suffering. Words are sounds emanating from someone's mouth, or they are pixels assembled on a computer screen. If you decline to form the opinion that these sounds or pixels are "offensive," then they have no intrinsic capacity to alter your mood or deprive you of equanimity. Take a moment, count to ten, or do something else to resist the reflexive impulse to take the words spoken in the way that the speaker wants them to be taken. It is irrational to allow a person who wishes to perturb you to succeed in doing so, and it is more irrational still to *assist* such a person's efforts to get under your skin and irritate you. The same is true of a person who strikes you. That person can, of course, damage your body, but you need not allow the imposition of damage to your body to have the additional effect of damaging your peace of mind or your serenity. You do not *have* to accept a slap to your face as an insult, but only as a slap to your face. If someone slaps you without justification, then the person committing the assault has degraded himself or herself. Another person's behavior does not have the power to make *you* less rational, less moral, or to degrade *your* character in any way. Insult or offense originates in *your* mind. The words or the blows come from the external world, but the damage to your *mind* is your fault. The world will do more than enough to try to damage you. There is no need to offer it your assistance. Other persons are free to speak of you as they choose and to believe about you whatever they will. You have only yourself to blame if you allow the beliefs and utterances of other persons to disturb you or throw you off balance emotionally or psychologically. What do you care about the goings-on inside of another person's head?

21. Let death and exile, and all other things which appear terrible be daily before your eyes, but chiefly death, and you win never entertain any abject thought, nor too eagerly covet anything.

Remind yourself on a daily basis that you are mortal, that everyone you love is mortal, and that everyone you have ever cared about is going to die sooner or later. The world, all of the evidence indicates, is rough on human bodies, and no one gets out of this world alive. This indicates two ineradicable facts about the human condition that apply to every person who has ever lived. First, death is the natural culmination of the process of being born and living a life. Mortality is not a *punishment*, nor is it something that ought to terrify those who are in possession of their faculties and disinclined to resist the inevitable. Second, your demise and the death of your loved ones are inevitable, and it is always irrational to allow yourself to become perturbed or upset about an event that you are certain *will* befall you. We all have to die, but we do *not* need to die in anguish or consumed by fear. Each of us is susceptible to potential "exile," in the form of imprisonment or some other condition that separates us from our loved ones. Even innocent people *can be* convicted and sentenced to life in prison. Ultimately you cannot control anyone else's judgment of your conduct, and that includes the possibility that false charges will be brought against you in court, and that a skilled prosecutor can convince the jury to convict you even if the charges are false. It *has* happened. In such a case, you will be "exiled" to a penitentiary, perhaps for the rest of your life. If this fate befalls you, the choice to remain emotionally stable is still open to you. You can, of course, become righteously indignant and howl lamentations against the courts, but that will not cause your prison to disintegrate, it is not particularly likely to earn you a retrial, and it will not ennoble you or make you a better person. Prison is probably not a place that you want to be, but it *is* possible to live a noble life even if you are behind bars. There are, in fact, "model prisoners," and there are honorable people in prison who manage to maintain their dignity despite their circumstances.

22. If you have an earnest desire of attaining to philosophy, prepare yourself from the very first to be laughed at, to be sneered by the multitude, to hear them say, "He is returned to us a philosopher all at once," and "Whence this supercilious look?" Now, for your part, don't have a supercilious look indeed; but keep steadily to those things which appear best to you as one appointed by God to this station. For remember that, if you adhere to the same point, those very persons who at first ridiculed will afterwards admire you. But if you are conquered by them, you will incur a double ridicule.

If you are sincere about wanting to acquire wisdom and virtue, you must be prepared to engage with the fact that some people will laugh at you and mock you, others will have no idea what you are trying to accomplish, and still others will treat you as if you believe that you are superior to them, or that you wish to be. You are likely to be derided, misunderstood, and resented. All of this can only bother you if you take it to heart, or if you regard the opinions and words of other persons as if they have some ability to prevent you from making genuine progress toward your most important goals. Remember that their words and opinions are *not* yours to control and that they are, therefore, none of your business. Remain untroubled by what goes on in someone else's head. What business, after all, is it of yours? Set about the task of pursuing wisdom as if you had been appointed to do so by God. Whether you *believe* in God is beside the point. Let the pursuit of wisdom be your central concern and the overarching project of your life's work. If ennobling your character is your primary goal, then you should not be thrown off track or impeded by the opinions of friends, family, or acquaintances. If you allow others to halt your progress toward admirable goals, then you will *deserve* their ridicule, and you will have failed at your quest, and you will have no one to blame but yourself, and no other cause to blame apart from your own indiscipline. Surely, you do not wish to turn the control of your mental states over to strangers or to the external world at large. Inviting others to rummage around inside your consciousness is libel to result in contamination of one sort or another.

23. If you ever happen to turn your attention to externals, so as to wish to please anyone, be assured that you have ruined your scheme of life. Be contented, then, in everything with being a philosopher; and, if you wish to be thought so likewise by anyone, appear so to yourself, and it will suffice you.

If you devote your time and energy to making money, acquiring power, gaining fame or notoriety, becoming more physically attractive, or to any other pursuit that does not contribute to your wisdom and virtue, then you have strayed from the narrow path leading to nobility and a flourishing life. There are likely to be temptations to indulge in these lesser pursuits, especially if persons among your family, friends, and community clamor for you to "make something of yourself," or to "live a normal life like everyone else." Your goals, however, should have nothing to do with becoming like those who live on the hedonic treadmill, or engage in the "rat race," or desire to "keep up with the Joneses." What is the great benefit of increasing your material possessions beyond necessity or garnering political or economic advantages, if you are not prepared to use those assets to improve your character and live a life worth living? A wealthy scoundrel is still a scoundrel. A powerful ignoramus is still an ignoramus. King Midas could turn objects to gold just by touching them, but look at what it cost him in the end because he lacked the wisdom to value his family more than mere gold. You must devote yourself to the types of pursuits that most people forgo in their unreflective quest for worldly goods that do not make them better people, and that many of them are willing to sacrifice their decency to attain. Their values are upside down and inside out. You must focus *solely* on wisdom, courage, justice, and self-discipline. Anything that does not facilitate those goals is useless to you. Why delve into an investigation of conditions that simply do not matter? This constitutes an easily avoidable waste of time and energy. Rest content with doing everything in your power to govern your mind, gain wisdom, and enhance your virtue. You do not need to receive applause for doing so, and you should not expect any.

24-a. Don't allow such considerations as these distress you. "I will live in dishonor, and be nobody anywhere." For, if dishonor is an evil, you can no more be involved in any evil by the means of another, than be engaged in anything base. Is it any business of yours, then, to get power, or to be admitted to an entertainment? By no means. How, then, after all, is this a dishonor? And how is it true that you will be nobody anywhere, when you ought to be somebody in those things only which are in your own control, in which you may be of the greatest consequence? "But my friends will be unassisted." — What do you mean by unassisted? They will not have money from you, nor will you make them Roman citizens. Who told you, then, that these are among the things in our own control, and not the affair of others?

No one can cause you to dishonor yourself so long as you conduct your mind, your behavior, and your affairs in honorable fashion. Nothing that anyone *says* about you or *does* to you can cause *you* to fall into dishonor, though they certainly risk their own character through misbehavior. If what they say about you is false and malicious, then they dishonor *themselves* by saying it. If they treat you roughly or inappropriately, and if the treatment is not rationally or morally unjustifiable, then they damage *their own* characters by mistreating an innocent person. You do not need political power, and you do not need to associate with celebrities or wealthy persons in order to pursue virtue. Do not worry that your career or your finances might suffer if you fail to develop the right "connections," or if you do not appease those who hold power. Their fame, wealth, and power are not proper objects of your concern. Indeed, these are not proper objects of *their* concern either, but that is no business of yours. Perhaps you will be unable to assist your friends and family if they should fall upon hard times, or if they desire some kind of benefit from the famous and powerful. Helping your family to get money and power is often useful, but it is not your primary function. A virtuous parent or spouse with little money is certainly preferable to having a wealthy *louse* in the house.

24-b. And who can give to another the things which he has not himself? "Well, but get them, then, that we too may have a share." If I can get them with the preservation of my own honor and fidelity and greatness of mind, show me the way and I will get them; but if you require me to lose my own proper good that you may gain what is not good, consider how inequitable and foolish you are.

Just as unwise people cannot impart wisdom to you, and people who lack virtue cannot transfer righteousness to your character, similarly you cannot provide wealth, fame, or power to those who lust after these things, if you do not control the mechanisms for acquiring such possessions. If a friend or a member of your family asks you to help in some business venture, or in some election campaign, then you are free to assist the person making the request, *provided that* you do *not* have to sacrifice your decency, your reason, or your honor in pursuing the project in question. If, however, your friend asks you to tell lies as part of a political campaign, or asks you to engage in underhanded tactics to smear an opponent in the race, then you *must* refuse to do so, and you should probably have nothing more to do with that person, as *that* is not the type of request a real friend makes. You may help one of your siblings with some business venture, but you may do so only insofar as no one asks you to indulge in corruption, dishonest dealing, or behavior that is detrimental to innocent persons or to the community at large. If your sibling asks you to, for example, conceal relevant information from inspectors or some regulatory body, then you *must* refuse and you must recognize that your sibling is behaving as an immoral person. Furthermore, do not forget the inherent limitations upon your time and energy. You do not know how much time you will be allotted, and you know that you have a great deal of work to do on improving your character. Do not fritter away either on a project that does not improve your rectitude. Press forward as if time is short. Accomplish what you can, but never trade away your integrity for mere material gain.

24-c. Besides, which would you rather have, a sum of money, or a friend of fidelity and honor? Rather assist me, then, to gain this character than require me to do those things by which I may lose it. Well, but my country, say you, as far as depends on me, will be unassisted. Here again, what assistance is this you mean? "It will not have porticoes nor baths of your providing." And what signifies that?

What kind of friend would ask you to lay aside your pursuit of wisdom, virtue, and self-improvement merely for the sake of helping that friend make some money, acquire a more powerful position, or obtain some trinket or other? Does this "friend" not understand that associating with honorable people who are loyal and trustworthy is far more valuable than anything that can be purchased with money or provided through a vote of the masses? Does this "friend" value your company only insofar as it proves useful to the satisfaction of goals other than your own? If your friend tells you that he wants to accomplish good deeds with his political power, or if she informs you that she intends to improve the community by putting the money to charitable purposes, then you can point out that good deeds can only flow from persons of good character, and you can note that charity may provide for material need, but it does not make the recipient wiser or more virtuous. Giving alms is all well and good, but it is no substitute for developing virtue. If your life is devoted to improving your character and attaining as much wisdom as you are capable of attaining, then these other concerns are not a proper part of your goals. Just as no one should expect to receive medical care from a painter, so should no one expect to get "porticos and baths," or parks and homeless shelters from a philosopher, or a seeker after wisdom. There are people who have chosen professions that are devoted to building the things that are physically necessary to a functioning society. If *you* did *not* choose such a profession, then you ought to work at the job you have chosen and you should not attempt to usurp someone else's proper role. Surely, it is good enough to serve as an example of honor, decency, and a life lived in accordance with nature and reason.

24-d. Why, neither does a smith provide it with shoes, or a shoemaker with arms. It is enough if everyone fully performs his own proper business. And were you to supply it with another citizen of honor and fidelity, would not he be of use to it? Yes. Therefore neither are you yourself useless to it. "What place, then, say you, will I hold in the state?" Whatever you can hold with the preservation of your fidelity and honor. But if, by desiring to be useful to that, you lose these, of what use can you be to your country when you are become faithless and void of shame.

There is a reasonable division of labor that ought to be sufficient to provide for all societal necessities, and each member of your society plays a role different from most of the others who do not work in the same field. It is not particularly useful or sensible to drive to the local tennis court if what you want is groceries with which to feed your family. Just as various people must perform their jobs properly if the grocery store is to be fully stocked and its goods available for purchase, so too there must be people who make it their business to understand wisdom and decency if they are to provide instruction to others, and to provide, also, an example of a flourishing, well-lived life. If you want to be a role model of admirable conduct, then you cannot spend your life working in professions that do not provide you the time or the opportunity to engage in the necessary studies and inquiries. Those who choose "practical" professions so as to supply their families with adequate food and shelter, or so as to provide their communities with civil engineering are doing their communities a valuable service. Such persons are certainly *not* to be denigrated. A society, however, in which those who are properly equipped to study wisdom choose, instead, to line their pockets with cash, or to devote their talents and time to feats of engineering, is a society that will find itself bereft of moral instruction and models of wisdom or decency. The world needs wisdom and virtue at least as much as it needs bridges and gutters. What good is crossing a bridge if doing so does not facilitate an enhancement of someone's virtue?

25-a. Is anyone preferred before you at an entertainment, or in a compliment, or in being admitted to a consultation? If these things are good, you ought to be glad that he has gotten them; and if they are evil, don't be grieved that you have not gotten them. And remember that you cannot, without using the same means [which others do] to acquire things not in our own control, expect to be thought worthy of an equal share of them.

There will be many occasions on which you will notice that some other person is receiving some form of preferential treatment from which you are, for whatever reason, excluded by the powers that be. If the preference in question is a genuine benefit, then you ought to be happy for the person receiving the advantage. What justification do you have for wanting to deprive another person of something that is good and advantageous? There is nothing virtuous about wanting other people to be deprived of good things or conditions that contribute to their well-being. If, on the other hand, the preferential treatment does *not* benefit the person receiving it, then you ought to be pleased that you are excluded from it. Why would you want to be treated in a manner that is not good for your character? It is masochistic to desire things or conditions that are harmful to the most important part of you. The benefit in question must not be subject to your control, otherwise you would simply produce it if you desired to do so, or you would prevent it from occurring if you thought that best. Given that the preferential treatment is *not* up to you, or subject to determination by your will, it follows that receiving it is *neither* good nor bad to you, because your own attainment of virtue is the only real good, and your falling into vice is the only real harm you can suffer. Thus, if you find that you are upset about a preference being granted to some other person, the reason for this is that you have lost sight of the true nature of the good. Envy is not good for your mind or your body. Try not to ruin your sleep and digestion with it. If you find that you envy some other person, the problem is probably *not* to be found in that other person's character.

25-b. For how can he who does not frequent the door of any [great] man, does not attend him, does not praise him, have an equal share with him who does? You are unjust, then, and insatiable, if you are unwilling to pay the price for which these things are sold, and would have them for nothing.

The only way to secure benefits and advantages from the wealthy, the famous, and the powerful is to flatter them, or to give them something that they want and cannot procure from anyone or anywhere else for the time being. What do you control that might appeal to the rich and the famous? Do they want you to pay attention to them and purchase their goods and services? Do the powerful want your vote and your campaign contributions? If they *deserved* or were entitled to your attention, then you would provide it to them spontaneously, and with no expectation of getting anything in return. A campaign contribution is not supposed to be a form of commerce, is it? If politicians were noble and admirable, then you would vote for them for morally legitimate reasons, and you could not expect anything in return other than wise governance and virtuous behavior in office. If, however, you donate money to a political campaign in the hope of winning favor and gaining a special degree of influence with a powerful or high-ranking person, then your contribution is an exercise in corruption, and you defile yourself by transferring money for nefarious purposes. As it happens, the people who gain favors from politicians, or bankers, or celebrities who influence the public, almost always acquire influence with these "movers and shakers" by giving them benefits, attention, votes, or just flat-out bribes that the powerful have done nothing legitimate to earn. The price of influencing powerful people so that they will provide you with some benefit or other *is* corruption. Are you willing to pay that price? If so, then you cannot *also* pursue noble or admirable goals. If you endeavor to be a successful flatterer of the powerful, then you relegate yourself to servility and dependence upon the generosity of a benefactor whom you do not control.

25-c. For how much is lettuce sold? Fifty cents, for instance. If another, then, paying fifty cents, takes the lettuce, and you, not paying it, go without them, don't imagine that he has gained any advantage over you. For as he has the lettuce, so you have the fifty cents which you did not give. So, in the present case, you have not been invited to such a person's entertainment, because you have not paid him the price for which a supper is sold. It is sold for praise; it is sold for attendance. Give him then the value, if it is for your advantage.

You would not expect to get free food from the grocery store, or free goods and services from your local mall. If you want a cake from the bakery, you can only obtain it if you pay the baker the price that he demands for it. It would be foolish and petulant to demand the cake for nothing, or to insist that the baker *must* supply the cake to you at *your* preferred price. You do not have the legitimate authority to set the price for goods that you do not currently own. You may *haggle*, perhaps, but *taking* the item for less than a price agreed upon by both parties is just theft. Similarly, if the Governor demands a massive contribution for throwing his support behind a piece of legislation or some socio-political agenda, then you are foolish if you insist that the politician *must* support your cause out of the goodness of her heart, or merely because it is the morally right thing to do. You are not dealing with a person who is particularly concerned about virtue and decency if that person issues you a *price* for the support that you seek. Either you make the corrupt politician a contribution, or perhaps tell the lies in public that the dishonest politician demands from you, or you must accept the fact that you are *not* going to get what you want, and you might want to consider whether your desires are properly calibrated. The alternative is to learn how to focus your energies, your wherewithal, and your other resources on the attainment of the honor and decency that you can produce simply by exerting your will. If this is your focus, then you simply will not care for anything that only the wealthy, and the powerful can provide.

25-d. But if you would, at the same time, not pay the one and yet receive the other, you are insatiable, and a blockhead. Have you nothing, then, instead of the supper? Yes, indeed, you have: the not praising him, whom you don't like to praise; the not bearing with his behavior at coming in.

If you insist upon having the wealthy, the famous, the powerful, and the influential give you the things that you ask of them, and if you also refuse to indulge in corruption, false flattery, or other illegal or immoral activities, then you are foolish and misguided. People who demand inappropriate conduct in exchange for illicit favors are not going to provide those favors if you refuse to satisfy their immoral demands. When, after all, is the last time that *you* did something that you disliked and felt no obligation to do so without deriving some benefit in exchange for the task? If you give to charity, or to some homeless person, do you not do so because you feel a moral obligation to help, or because you derive some form of pleasure from being charitable and beneficent to the needy? Suppose that you recognize no such obligation, you do not feel proud of yourself or good about yourself for helping those in need, and you see no other benefit to handing out alms for the poor. Clearly, you would *not* do it under those circumstances. We do not act voluntarily without some kind of reason, some kind of motivation, or without forming some intention or other. People who demand that you praise them, whether you believe that they are *worthy* of praise or not, are simply not the kind of people that are going to be motivated by altruism, moral obligations, or anything other than self-aggrandizement, profit, and vanity. If you want something from such a person, then you will have to pay the price he demands. You will have to do something discreditable or dishonorable. Of course, you do not *have* to want *anything* that the corrupt happen to control. Do you *really* want to gain material benefit from corruption? This is an ignoble desire, is it not? Try to avoid degrading yourself even further as you bow and scrape for your benefactor's delight.

26. The will of nature may be learned from those things in which we don't distinguish from each other. For example, when our neighbor's boy breaks a cup, or the like, we are presently ready to say, "These things will happen." Be assured, then, that when your own cup likewise is broken, you ought to be affected just as when another's cup was broken. Apply this in like manner to greater things. Is the child or wife of another dead? There is no one who would not say, "This is a human accident," but if anyone's own child happens to die, it is presently, "Alas I how wretched am I!" But it should be remembered how we are affected in hearing the same thing concerning others.

All persons share a common humanity, and all of us are members of the same confused primate species trying to make our way on the same planet facing, more or less, the same challenges as the other people. It is not terribly difficult to identify all sorts of tendencies that we have in common, but if we pay attention, then we will notice how we are disposed to behave differently to challenges and difficulties that others face, as opposed to the manner in which we tend to behave when *we* are faced with similar types of circumstances afflicting our *own* lives. Given that we share the human condition in common, it is irrational to treat our own problems as if they are more terrible when they afflict ourselves, than when the same type of problem befalls a neighbor or coworker. Notice how easy it is for you to bear damage to your neighbor's car or home. You tell yourself, "These kinds of things are bound to happen," and you are correct to do so. If *your* car, however, is damaged in a fashion that is equivalent to the damage your neighbor's car has suffered, or if you find the same infestation of termites has befallen *your* home, then you get far more upset because *you* have to write the check to repair the vehicle or pay the exterminator. You cannot have it both ways. A damaged car is either something significant and constitutes a condition worthy of relinquishing your peace of mind, or it is *not*. The same rule applies to the more formidable challenges. The death of a child is not inherently worse if it is *your child*. Everyone is, after all, *someone's* child. This is difficult to deny.

27. As a mark is not set up for the sake of missing the aim, so neither does the nature of evil exist in the world.

According to a variety of sources, the word "sin" is derived from the ancient art of archery. When an archer was guilty of missing the mark and, according to *some* commentators on the matter, ruining the arrow so that it could not be fired again, the archer had "sinned" and had failed in his central purpose as an archer. The target is not set up for the purpose of getting the archer to *miss* it, or for *ruining* the very arrow shot at it. It would be far easier to miss the target if no target had been erected in the first place, would it not? No, the purpose of erecting a target in an archery competition, or a trapshooting tournament, is to offer the competitors something that they can attempt to *hit*. Imagine the foolishness of attempting to play a basketball game with *no hoop*. The hoop only exists for the sake of allowing players to put a basketball through it, and professional players who shoot and miss have failed to do what they get *paid* to do. When it comes to perpetrating evil, or committing a "sin," the perpetrator misses the mark and fails to do what nature provides the opportunity to do. The human race is endowed with the faculty of reason, and the capacity to use that faculty to determine those actions that are in accordance with reason and the natural gifts with which human beings are endowed, as opposed to those actions that are *contrary* to the natural order. The non-human animals do not perpetrate evil, and cannot be held morally accountable for their behavior, precisely because they lack the capacity to reason about the nature of good and evil. Evil, therefore, is not *inherent* in the natural world, but is rather part and parcel of the act of misusing reason, or failing to behave in accordance with the dictates of reason as the essence of human nature. Evil comes into being because human beings miss the mark. The natural world does not perpetrate evil deeds. Lions may kill their prey, but they certainly do not *murder* their prey. *People* bring evil into the world.

28. If a person gave your body to any stranger he met on his way, you would certainly be angry. And do you feel no shame in handing over your own mind to be confused and mystified by anyone who happens to verbally attack you?

If you were enslaved or imprisoned without just cause, then you would be outraged, you would protest, and everyone would understand your predicament and would understand the injustice that had been done to you. There are good reasons that murder, rape, and assault are each regarded as among the worst deeds that a malefactor can perpetrate against a victim. Bodily autonomy is generally regarded as sacrosanct, and encroachments upon your body are to be resisted with all of your might, and they are to be punished in proportion to the damage done to you. You would *never* allow an assault upon your body to go unanswered or unchallenged. Why, then, would you *ever* allow anyone to control the direction of your mind, which is the proper function or your reason as your ruling faculty, by saying a few words, making a gesture with his hands, or contorting his face in one way as opposed to another? Why would you allow your mind to be imprisoned or captured by some stranger? It is the height of irrationality to allow another person to dictate your mood, or to compel you to adopt an infelicitous frame of mind, simply because that person has made a particular series of noises with his face, or because of the tone of voice. If you pay even the slightest attention, then you will surely notice that people frequently get angry because of a few words that they hear or read. Other people will become ecstatic because of flattery, or because of a response to a marriage proposal. Of course, these same people will become despondent if the marriage proposal is declined, or if the flattery is replaced with criticism. Can you not see how foolish and weak-minded you have to be in order to allow other people to impose this or that mental state upon you with a few words or gestures? Can you not "captain your own soul," and ignore such silliness on the part of others? Do not hand your serenity over to another person.

29-a. In every affair consider what precedes and follows, and then undertake it. Otherwise you will begin with spirit; but not having thought of the consequences, when some of them appear you will shamefully desist. "I would conquer at the Olympic games." But consider what precedes and follows, and then, if it is for your advantage, engage in the affair.

When you set a goal, you must try to understand as much as you are able about all that will be required of you if you are to attain the goal you have set. It is one thing to form a desire for a certain event to transpire, but it is something far more complex and difficult to rouse the willingness to do whatever will prove to be necessary in order to accomplish your goal and bring the desired event to fruition. Any child can say, "I want to win the Olympic gold medal in wrestling," but *very* few will ever attain that goal, because the vast majority are either unable or unwilling to subject themselves to the rigorous training and the many hardships that are necessary to become an Olympic caliber wrestler. Most people will quit rather than put themselves through the years, perhaps decades, of practice and preparation that Olympians must endure. If you set a goal, and then you fail to attain that goal, not because your best efforts were insufficient, but rather because you proved to be *unwilling* to exert your best efforts over the long-term, then *that* is the essence of failure. That is a failure of will, a failure of self-discipline, and a failure of fortitude. It is a failure of *character*. Losing a wrestling match, or any other competition, to a superior opponent is neither shameful nor is it a catastrophe. You cannot control your opponent's skills, or your opponent's will. You cannot control circumstances such as injuries or the decision of the judges. You can, however, control your *dedication* to accomplishing the task at hand. The only true failure is the failure to do everything in your power to succeed. Having done your very best is the essence of success, whether you get the gold medal or not. Gold is, after all, nothing more than a mineral. Chasing after the gold medal, merely for the *sake* of the gold medal, will probably prove insufficient to sustain the effort required to capture it. You must also wish to make something greater of *yourself.*

29-b. You must conform to rules, submit to a diet, refrain from dainties; exercise your body, whether you choose it or not, at a stated hour, in heat and cold; you must drink no cold water, nor sometimes even wine. In a word, you must give yourself up to your master, as to a physician.

If you want to achieve a physical goal, then you *must* be willing to adopt a specified diet, and to adopt an exercise regimen, and to subject yourself to whatever extremes of heat, cold, altitude, and any other necessary environmental conditions. You will not be able to eat sweets or indulge in drugs or alcohol, and you must refrain from any and all activities that could be detrimental to your performance within the arena *you* have chosen. Furthermore, you must be willing to subordinate your will to the direction of your coaches, trainers, nutritionists, and other experts without whom you will be unable to perform at the highest levels of which you are capable with their guidance. You cannot be headstrong or arrogant and still expect to make genuine progress. Look to those people who have been working and training competitors within your chosen discipline for many years, and look to those who have demonstrated that they know how to help their students succeed. If your coach orders you to jog ten miles backward, then it is not your place to refuse to do so or even to question *why* you were given this order. It is by virtue of obedience to masters and high-performance trainers that you are able to advance, improve, and attain the greatest heights of which you are capable. The greatest performers have always subjected themselves to years of excruciating training, and they have always been willing to do the things that lesser competitors were either unwilling or unable to force themselves to do. Probably, no one wins an Olympic gold medal without years of unyielding *dedication*. If someone manages to win Olympic gold *without* that kind of dedication, then that person is probably the genetic equivalent of a super hero.

29-c. Then, in the combat, you may be thrown into a ditch, dislocate your arm, turn your ankle, swallow dust, be whipped, and, after all, lose the victory. When you have evaluated all this, if your inclination still holds, then go to war. Otherwise, take notice, you will behave like children who sometimes play like wrestlers, sometimes gladiators, sometimes blow a trumpet, and sometimes act a tragedy when they have seen and admired these shows.

No matter what you do for a living, or what style of life you choose to lead, you can be certain that the world is going to put you to the test, challenge your capacity to remain calm, and set your contentment on the chopping block. There will be trials, difficulties, setbacks, failures, and you will suffer damage to your body as well as to your ego. Knowing this, are you willing to wade forward into the dangers and subject yourself to every danger with which you may be presented? Remember that if you choose to enter into combat, then you must also be willing to choose putting yourself at risk, and subjecting yourself to injuries and to defeat at your opponent's hands. Do nothing halfheartedly. You must *dedicate* yourself to the task at hand in both body and soul, or you must not engage in the combat at all. Do not behave like children who play at being soldiers one day, then pretend to be firefighters the next, and pretend to be rock stars the day after that. Playacting is all well and good for children, but it is not appropriate for adults who pursue noble goals. Too many adults go through life without any overarching values, projects, and guiding principles. This is also childish behavior. Identify your most fundamental values, decide what kind of person you want to become, and set doggedly about doing what is necessary to develop the kind of character that you will need to accomplish your goals. If you are not prepared to brave whatever challenges may arise, then you are not prepared to pursue lofty goals. It is rare that any *significant* achievement is easily realized. You must be prepared to withstand anything that the world throws at you and you must persevere doggedly if you intend to accomplish anything worthy of a decent person's pursuit.

29-d. Thus you too will be at one time a wrestler, at another a gladiator, now a philosopher, then an orator; but with your whole soul, nothing at all. Like an ape, you mimic all you see, and one thing after another is sure to please you, but is out of favor as soon as it becomes familiar. For you have never entered upon anything considerately, nor after having viewed the whole matter on all sides, or made any scrutiny into it, but rashly, and with a cold inclination.

Your life must have a *central* purpose if you are to avoid the fate of becoming a dilettante who dabbles in a variety of disciplines but attains greatness and true mastery in *none* of them. Actors must play many different roles as they appear in different productions and adhere to different scripts. Even actors, however, when rehearsal and shooting wrap up, have to go back to real life, and they must face the same question, "Who am I, *really*?" that everyone else must consider and attempt to answer. If you are *not* an actor, then you ought to be prepared to answer that question with a description of an adult with an immutable set of values. Unless your will is set in stone, you will find that you are unable to rise to the challenge of hardship and struggle. You will find that you are unable to resist temptation. You will find that you wander easily off of the path to wisdom and virtue to chase the useless "shiny things" that distract children. If you choose *not* to devote your life to a single overarching goal, then you will end up playacting at many different short-lived fantasies, and you will need to adopt a different persona for each one. You will, in some sense, never have a genuine identity. That is no way for an adult to live. Playing at an endeavor until you become bored with it, and then switching your attentions to something else, *that* is not a rational or cohesive style of life. Devote your life, the *entire* project, to becoming a wise and virtuous adult. What higher and nobler goal can you imagine? There is no goal more worthy of your time, energy, and effort than being honorable and upstanding.

29-e. Thus some, when they have seen a philosopher and heard a man speaking like Euphrates (though, indeed, who can speak like him?), have a mind to be philosophers too. Consider first, man, what the matter is, and what your own nature is able to bear. If you would be a wrestler, consider your shoulders, your back, your thighs; for different persons are made for different things. Do you think that you can act as you do, and be a philosopher? That you can eat and drink, and be angry and discontented as you are now?

Many people see someone performing as a virtuoso, or astonishing the crowd with athleticism, or holding forth in stupendous oratory that keeps the crowd rapt and on the edges of their seats, and they fancy themselves capable of doing the same things as the specialists whom they behold. How many of them, however, have thought carefully about all that will be required of them before they can ever attain the heights of human performance that they have witnessed and upon which they have marveled? If you hope to play in the National Basketball Association someday, then you had better be genetically endowed with great height, a hyper-efficient cardiovascular system, and tremendous hand-eye coordination. Without these gifts, you will never make it as a professional basketball player or, at the very least, you will never attain greatness approaching that exhibited by Michael Jordan or Larry Bird. Setting your goals upon wisdom and virtue is no lesser an attainment than is becoming a professional or Olympic caliber athlete. You cannot maintain the same behavioral proclivities and the same undisciplined patterns of thought that you have now, and still hope to develop the self-discipline of a Socrates or an Epictetus. You will have to put aside common interests and typical concerns. If you are not willing to turn away from the usual worldly concerns and material pursuits, then you will never make progress toward unwavering imperturbability.

To be an "Olympian of Virtue" is no mean feat, and you must be prepared to do whatever is required for you to rise to such heights.

29-f. You must watch, you must labor, you must get the better of certain appetites, must quit your acquaintance, be despised by your servant, be laughed at by those you meet; come off worse than others in everything, in magistracies, in honors, in courts of judicature.

Be prepared to cut off all of your associations with people who do not bring out the best in your behavior, and all of those who do not exhibit any interest in virtuous character or the attainment of wisdom. Anyone who does not understand what you are trying to accomplish, and all of those who regard your pursuit of more admirable character as something laughable, all such persons can *only* serve as stumbling blocks along your way and impediments to your progress. You would do well to be rid of such persons and their company once and for all. You must prepare yourself to be regarded as pretentious, foolish, out of touch, and as a generally worthless figure by new persons whom you encounter. Most people will think that you are wasting your life, or that you are simply pretending to be something that you are not, or that you ought to share goals similar to those pursued by the masses. Their beliefs, and their assessments of your overarching project are nothing that should concern you and nothing worthy of your emulation. If you are not willing to withstand the "slings and arrows" hurled at you by the common person who thinks that only money, sex, power, and fame are worth chasing, then you will never have the fortitude to face constant criticism and ceaseless struggle without losing your peace of mind, and without wavering where your quest is concerned. Be content for the people you meet to judge you to be an inferior, or a ludicrous person of no account. When others point at you and laugh, you must have the mental discipline to remain unaffected by their jeers. You must turn your back on common pursuits if you wish to achieve uncommon goals. If you set your sights on a mountain summit, then you will have to leave the common comforts of flatlands.

29-g. When you have considered all these things round, approach, if you please; if, by parting with them, you have a mind to purchase equanimity, freedom, and tranquility. If not, don't come here; don't, like children, be one while a philosopher, then a publican, then an orator, and then one of Caesar's officers. These things are not consistent. You must be one man, either good or bad. You must cultivate either your own ruling faculty or externals, and apply yourself either to things within or without you; that is, be either a philosopher, or one of the vulgar.

Only when you have weighed up and contemplated everything that will be required of you, and only when you are completely resigned to confront *any* challenge with which you may be presented, *only* then are you prepared to begin your pursuit of wisdom, virtue, and a flourishing life. If you are *not* prepared to give *everything* that you have, and every iota of fortitude that you *will* have to this quest, and if you are not prepared to divest yourself of anything that is incompatible with your pursuits, including the people with whom you have spent most of your life until now, then you are not prepared to take up the study of philosophy, the pursuit of wisdom, or of virtue, or of decency in earnest. Without this level of commitment, you will behave like a child who wants to be an astronaut until he finds out that being an astronaut requires learning a lot of math and physics. You do not want to end up like the adolescent who wants to become a veterinarian because she likes dogs and horses, but then finds out that she is not prepared for the rigorous study of the various very complex biological sciences that she must master if she is to get through all of the necessary schooling. Adults really ought not latch on to vague dreams without understanding the many obstacles to which those dreams are subject and the totality of training and discipline that will be required if their dreams are to be fulfilled. Adults should not think or behave like children. Is it not long since time for you to have "put away childish things" and to have made a virtuous adult of yourself?

30. Duties are universally measured by relations. Is anyone a father? If so, it is implied that the children should take care of him, submit to him in everything, patiently listen to his reproaches, his correction. But he is a bad father. Are you naturally entitled, then, to a good father? No, only to a father. Is a brother unjust? Well, keep your own situation towards him. Consider not what he does, but what you are to do to keep your own faculty of choice in a state conformable to nature. For another will not hurt you unless you please. You will then be hurt when you think you are hurt. In this manner, therefore, you will find, from the idea of a neighbor, a citizen, a general, the corresponding duties if you accustom yourself to contemplate the several relations.

No one is entitled to perfect parents, perfect children, perfect siblings, or any other form of perfect familial relation. Indeed, no one is entitled to be *born at all* much less entitled to be born as a member of the human species that Aristotle called the "rational animal." If your parents treat you poorly, then your obligation is to learn how to respond to parental mistreatment in a rational, honorable, and admirable fashion. Even a bad father is a father, even a bad mother is a mother, and even a bad brother or sister deserves your respect insofar as family members are concerned, because you have a special relationship with these persons that you can never have with anyone else. Do not respond to incompetent parenting by being an ungrateful, petulant child. Do not become a bad sibling just because one or more of your siblings mistreats you. Never use any family member's mistakes or poor conduct as an excuse for you to become a terrible member of the family, or for you to conduct yourself inappropriately toward any member of your kinfolk. Remember that your character can only be harmed or damaged by *your own* conduct. No one else can cause you to become a liar, a coward, or an ingrate. You are the only person who is capable of degrading *your* character. The manner in which others treat you has no purchase on your uprightness. Let others misbehave if they must, but do not join them in their self-abasement. Remember that those who mistreat you cannot harm you, but can only degrade *themselves*. Do not respond to their self-degradation by indulging in your own.

31-a. Be assured that the essential property of piety towards the gods is to form right opinions concerning them, as existing "I and as governing the universe with goodness and justice. And fix yourself in this resolution, to obey them, and yield to them, and willingly follow them in all events, as produced by the most perfect understanding."

Whether you believe in God or not, it is advisable to conduct yourself *as if* an omniscient, omnipotent, and perfectly benevolent deity is watching you and judging your conduct so as to mete out justice in this life or in the next. In this way, you will do everything in your power to make rational decisions and engage in virtuous, ennobling behavior. If there *is* a just God, then your behavior will please God, and if there is no God, then you will manage yourself in admirable fashion, and you will experience virtue as its own reward. You will make a *better* human being of yourself. You will not become bitter about events as they transpire if you attribute them to God's will or if you understand that events unfold as the laws of nature dictate. What sense is there in blaming nature for anything? Nature cannot do anything other than the laws of nature dictate. If there is a God who created and designed the cosmos, then you certainly have no business second guessing your Creator or complaining about the universe that God has created so that you can enjoy the opportunity to live a human life. Those who allow themselves to become bitter and disappointed with their lives are rejecting the world as it stands, and this indicates an ungrateful and irrational petulance. Whether you embrace events as they unfold or you complain and resist the circumstances that you encounter, the world *is* going to have its way with you. The world is large, *you* are small, and your life is just one tiny series of events within the vastly larger set of unfolding occurrences that is the universe. Who do you think you are? How did you get the impression that the world has to conform to your whims and desires? Whether there is or is not a God, you can be very confident that *you* are not in charge of the world. In fact, you are probably not even in charge of your *neighborhood*.

31-b. For thus you will never find fault with the gods, nor accuse them as neglecting you. And it is not possible for this to be effected any other way than by withdrawing yourself from things not in our own control, and placing good or evil in those only which are.

The only good or bad circumstances that can ever befall you are those conditions that you determine by the exertion of your own will or your faculty of deliberation and choice. There is nothing that anyone can do to you, not even "the gods," that can either improve your character or undermine your integrity. In this area, you are sovereign and no other person, no other power, has the capacity to compel you to engage in any vice. If you behave in an inappropriate fashion, then you have only yourself to blame for the misdeed and the damage to your decency. Do not disingenuously accuse circumstance or other persons. Similarly, when you do the right thing, and do it for the morally correct reason, then you are thereby ennobled and you improve your character through *your own* efforts. Other persons and external events can damage your body, your property, your reputation, or your family, but none of these are entirely within your control, and damage to them is not tantamount to damage to your decency or your integrity. When you consider what things are good and what things are evil, you *must* look *only* to your own thoughts and actions because you can only be morally responsible for those things that you can control. Remember also that those conditions that do *not* lie within your control are, therefore, conditions that lie outside the sphere of your control and ought to lie outside the sphere of your *concern*. If your nation or its political leaders misbehave, then this is no fault of yours, as you do not have the power to make them behave otherwise. If *you* misbehave, then only *you* are responsible. Let the rest of the world govern itself, and you look to *your own* governance.

It is typically good advice to *mind your own business*. If you are devoting the necessary time and energy to self-rectification, then you should have little of either left over to devote to the quixotic quest of world domination.

31-c. For if you suppose any of the things not in our own control to be either good or evil, when you are disappointed of what you wish, or incur what you would avoid, you must necessarily find fault with and blame the authors. For every animal is naturally formed to fly and abhor things that appear hurtful, and the causes of them; and to pursue and admire those which appear beneficial, and the causes of them.

Many people make the mistake of blaming others or blaming circumstances when they do not get what they want or when they incur conditions that they want to avoid. They blame their unsatisfied desires and their realized aversions on someone or something other than themselves. This is *always* an error. If you restrict your desires to those things that *only* you can control, then no one has the power to deprive you of the satisfaction of your desires. For example, if you want to be an honorable spouse who does not commit adultery, then you simply refuse to indulge in adulterous behavior, and no one can force you to behave in contrary fashion. If you are averse to being a thief or a coward, then you have only yourself to blame should you find that you have committed an act of theft or allowed yourself to succumb to cowardice. It is impossible for anyone else to make a thief or a coward of you. Do not make the mistake of desiring wealth, because if you adopt that irrational desire, then you will become angry with persons or circumstances that you perceive as preventing you from acquiring the money that you want. Money is not a proper object of a rational and virtuous person's desires. You can be deprived of wealth in many different ways but the deprivation of wealth is not an evil, just as the acquisition of wealth is not a good. A wealthy man who disgraces himself by engaging in vicious conduct is an evil man in spite of his wealth, and an impoverished man who ennobles himself with virtue is both *morally* better, and better off, than an evil man. No condition external to your will and your conduct can make you into a better or a worse human being. The world has never been yours to control. Govern your own behavior within the world. *That* will have to be enough to keep you busy.

31-d. It is impractical, then, that one who supposes himself to be hurt should be happy about the person who, he thinks, hurts him, just as it is impossible to be happy about the hurt itself. Hence, also, a father is reviled by a son, when he does not impart to him the things which he takes to be good; and the supposing empire to be a good made Polynices and Eteocles mutually enemies. On this account the husbandman, the sailor, the merchant, on this account those who lose wives and children, revile the gods.

If you believe that someone else has harmed you, ask yourself whether his or her actions have damaged your *character*, or is the alleged "damage" merely applicable to your wealth, your reputation, or your property? Someone who crashes into your car and causes significant damage to your vehicle and your body does not, thereby, injure your integrity or your decency. The car can be fixed or replaced, and your good does not reside in the condition of your possessions. Your automobile does not *have* integrity, dignity, or other moral properties. Perhaps your body can be repaired, and perhaps it cannot, but your body is not a repository of your virtue either. If you are a decent and admirable human being, then you do not become less honorable merely because you are confined to a hospital bed or a wheelchair. If you allow yourself to believe that your house, your car, your bank account, or even your family constitute your *good*, then you will become enraged at anyone who damages any of these. The world, of course, will have its way with everything that is *not* yours to control. The anger you experience when this happens will be *your* fault entirely, because you made the mistake of allowing your desires and aversions to attach to events, conditions, and things that lie beyond the control of your will. Even an Emperor (such as Marcus Aurelius) does not really control the empire. If that were the case, then no empire would ever collapse. Similarly, the parent does not really control the family and its well-being. If that were the case, then your loved ones would never die. Never *insist* that the world *must* be other than it is. Who, after all, authorized *you* to govern the world?

31-e. For where interest is, there too is piety placed. So that, whoever is careful to regulate his desires and aversions as he ought, is, by the very same means, careful of piety likewise. But it is also incumbent on everyone to offer libations and sacrifices and first fruits, conformably to the customs of his country, with purity, and not in a slovenly manner, nor negligently, nor sparingly, nor beyond his ability.

Think of the direction and governance of your desires and aversions as exercises in piety and as moral and rational *obligations*. Just as persons who are sincere about their religious faith take all religious commitments very seriously, so too should you dedicate yourself to doing everything in your power to govern yourself in rational and honorable fashion. Pursue your own decency with the equivalent of religious zealotry. You are obligated to pursue the good with everything that you have, and to devote just as much energy and commitment to avoiding vice at all costs. If there is any behavior that a good and just God would frown upon, then avoid that behavior whether you believe in God or not. You do not need a God to reward you for just conduct, because justice and virtue are their own rewards. You ennoble your character by conducting yourself in virtuous fashion. Similarly, you have no need for a God to punish you if you engage in vicious or "sinful" behavior. You impose punishment upon yourself every time that you do something that is discreditable or that is unworthy of a decent human being. That kind of behavior degrades your character (or your *soul*), and there is no way to escape *that* damage. Why would you want to degrade yourself by becoming a liar, a cheat, a thief, or any other type of person that is unworthy of respect? Whether you "get caught" in the misdeed in question, and whether you are "brought to justice" by either human courts or by God, *you* will know what you have done, and *your* character will suffer for the vice you commit. *Why* would you do any such thing to yourself? Have enough respect for yourself and for decency to do everything you can to be virtuous. There is *no* more important object of your concern.

32-a. When you have recourse to divination, remember that you know not what the event will be, and you come to learn it of the diviner; but of what nature it is you know before you come, at least if you are a philosopher. For if it is among the things not in our own control, it can by no means be either good or evil.

Whatever fate may have in store for you, whatever challenges happenstance may hurl in your path or, if you are a believer, whatever God presents you with, remember that you always have the ability to deal with events in a rational, honorable, and virtuous fashion. If the world presents you with a challenge or a difficult circumstance, then you must determine what component of the condition with which you are presented lies within the control of your will, and what elements are beyond your control. If you hear a rumor that the company by which you are employed is headed for bankruptcy, and your employment will cease to be available to you in the near future, then you cannot change the financial circumstances of the corporation, but you *can* certainly plan for the possible dissolution of your employer, and you can maintain your rational self-governance irrespective of any economic circumstances or conditions of your employment or unemployment. Should your nation be hit by a recession, or even a depression, it will not be in your power to dispel or to alter the condition of the nation's economy, but *nothing* can deprive you of your capacity to retain your dignity and your honor whatever the material fates may throw your way. You should not, therefore, be troubled by *any* news you may hear, no matter what the source of the information may be, for it is always within your power to take the news of the day, dissect it like a rational adult in possession of your faculties, respond to the news in accordance with the dictates of reason, and no one can compel you to sacrifice your peace of mind just because others may panic. When has panic ever engendered your best decisions and your best behavior? Panic is not a good strategy for improving yourself, your circumstances, or your prospects for the future. Panic is, in fact, not a good strategy for accomplishing *anything*.

32-b. Don't, therefore, bring either desire or aversion with you to the diviner (else you will approach him trembling), but first acquire a distinct knowledge that every event is indifferent and nothing to you, of whatever sort it may be, for it will be in your power to make a right use of it, and this no one can hinder; then come with confidence to the gods, as your counselors, and afterwards, when any counsel is given you, remember what counselors you have assumed, and whose advice you will neglect if you disobey.

Never approach any report of the news or of your probable future circumstances with the attitude that the news or those who may report it to you have the power to strip you of your equanimity or to direct your response to the news of the day. They have *no* such power and *never* can have it. Remind yourself that no circumstance beyond your control can be an evil or a catastrophe for you, and also that no condition that is *not* determined by your faculty of deliberation and choice can make you a better (or worse) person. Maintain your rationally grounded indifference to all external events, and remember that you are ultimately in control of your attitude, your desires and aversions, and your state of mind, and *no* external events can alter this fact. In this way you can retain your confidence no matter what the news of the day may be, no matter what anyone predicts for the near or distant future, and no matter what alleged benefit or detriment anyone holds out for your consideration. If you are presented with reason to believe that you are going to die in the near future, then you have the ability to settle whatever affairs are within your control and, more importantly, the fortitude to approach death with the resolve and serenity appropriate to a reasoning being. You have been provided with the wisest counsel that posterity has had to offer, and you can blame no one else if you fail to heed the wise counsel you have been given.

As for counsel that is *unwise,* shame on you if you mistake that for genuine wisdom and act in accordance with the will of the common person or the masses. Do you aim to be *common*? There is certainly nothing particularly admirable about *that.*

32-c. Come to divination, as Socrates prescribed, in cases of which the whole consideration relates to the event, and in which no opportunities are afforded by reason, or any other art, to discover the thing proposed to be learned. When, therefore, it is our duty to share the danger of a friend or of our country, we ought not to consult the oracle whether we will share it with them or not.

If you face a condition in which all of the available evidence and the most careful application of your reason does not provide you with an obviously preferable choice, and if you face a choice that is forced and unavoidable, then you may have to rely upon some other source to assist your deliberations concerning what you ought to do. You may, on many occasions, *have* to choose without knowing everything that you would like to know. What, for example, should you believe about the probable future of your nation, your culture, and the prospects for the next few generations? It is, at least arguably, impossible to predict the likely future of the economy, the environment, the likely developments in technological advancements, or the future availability of various natural resources. Nonetheless, you cannot *avoid* choices and behaviors that will impact your circumstances, and the material well-being of any offspring you may have, or of any future generations that will be impacted by your decisions. What should you do with your limited time and resources given that you cannot *know* the best or most felicitous practical expenditures of your energies over the long-term? If you seek advice from experts or from those who claim access to information that is not available to you, then you are obligated to use the available testimony in a manner that is virtuous and beneficial to those with whom you share familial and cultural relations. Do not conceal information that may be of genuine benefit to your fellow citizens. There may, however, be occasions on which your natural inclinations are the only foundation you have for choosing one course as opposed to another. In such cases, when some form of action is necessary, you must be willing to choose, and you must be prepared to embrace whatever consequences ensue from your decision.

32-d. For, though the diviner should forewarn you that the victims are unfavorable, this means no more than that either death or mutilation or exile is portended. But we have reason within us, and it directs, even with these hazards, to the greater diviner, the Pythian god, who cast out of the temple the person who gave no assistance to his friend while another was murdering him.

You need not fear predictions of your demise, because you have known for many years that you are mortal and that your life in this body does not last forever. Perhaps there is some form of life after bodily death, and perhaps there is not, but it is fairly clear that your body *will* expire. Similarly, you need not panic at the possibility that your body may suffer illness, injury, imprisonment, or even torture, because you have long known that all human bodies, including your own, are subject to various forms of damage, manhandling, dismemberment, and ultimate dissolution. It is not "news" to you that the world tends to damage the human frame and, ultimately, kill it. The human body is frail, the world is large and powerful, and there is no indication that the world is likely to treat your body with kid gloves, or to allow you to escape this "vale of tears" unscathed. No matter what dangers you may face, it is advisable for you to remember that your reason and your character are *always* yours to control, and the only evil that can befall you is degradation that you impose upon your own rectitude through irrationality and misbehavior, whereas the only good you can experience is ennobling thought and conduct that you personify and embody in virtuous fashion. If you have a friend or family member who is being threatened or who stands in the path of potential danger, then you are obligated, as a friend and as a decent human being, to do everything in your power to prevent an injustice from occurring, and to stand athwart any attempt to impose undeserved damage to innocent persons. If you wish to be honorable, then you must *behave* honorably and you must especially do so when dangers arise. Be assured, dangers *will* arise. *Always* be prepared.

33-a. Immediately prescribe some character and form of conduct to yourself, which you may keep both alone and in company.

Identify your core values and do not deviate from conducting yourself in accordance with those values under *any* circumstances. Furthermore, it is absolutely crucial that you *never* behave differently in private than you do in public. A person of genuine character does not present one face when a large group of people is watching, but another when only one or two people are present or when that person is alone. If you abhor dishonesty, then you must tell the truth, or at least avoid lying, no matter what the consequences, and no matter how many people may or may not be listening. If you believe that stealing is evil, then you are *never* permitted to steal, no matter what your circumstances, even if you know that you can "get away" with theft and avoid the justice of the courts, and even if you stand to gain more money than most can even imagine. No amount of money is worth the sacrifice of your decency. You either believe that theft is evil or you do not. If you even take contingencies into serious consideration, then you are not an adult genuinely devoted to decency and honor. Do not allow yourself to indulge in excuses where core values are concerned, and make certain that you identify behaviors that are *never* excusable and in which you will *never* engage, even if the heavens fall as a result. If *any* circumstance could *ever* cause you to violate your principles, then you have no business referring to "principles" at all. Is there anything that could convince you to commit murder, which is the act of killing a human being without just cause? If there is any concatenation of events that might persuade you to commit *murder*, then do not pretend that you oppose murder and do not pretend to be a morally upstanding human being. Evil is *not* subject to *any* contingency. You must avoid perpetrating evil irrespective of circumstance. Do not pretend and do not invent excuses for vice. Hold yourself to a higher standard than *that*.

33-b. Be for the most part silent, or speak merely what is necessary, and in few words. We may, however, enter, though sparingly, into discourse sometimes when occasion calls for it, but not on any of the common subjects, of gladiators, or horse races, or athletic champions, or feasts, the vulgar topics of conversation; but principally not of men, so as either to blame, or praise, or make comparisons. If you are able, then, by your own conversation bring over that of your company to proper subjects; but, if you happen to be taken among strangers, be silent.

The old adage, attributed to many different sources, that we have only one mouth but two ears and this is nature's way, or God's way, of telling us that we should listen twice as often as we speak, constitutes wise and valuable advice. You will learn much more from listening than you will ever learn from speaking. You do not learn a great deal while running your mouth. When you *do* have legitimate occasion to speak, you would do well to avoid topics such as sports, entertainment, trivial political partisanship, or gossip. None of these are ennobling expenditures of your time and energy. It is usually inappropriate to affix praise, blame, or to compare the exploits of various persons. The conduct and utterances of other persons is *not* your business, and you would do well to focus on improving your *own* character and comportment, which is not accomplished by speaking either well or ill of others. Especially when you find that you are surrounded by strangers, it is wise to keep quiet as much as possible, because you probably do not know their motives or the general direction that the conversation is likely to go. On other occasions, you may be able to influence the course of conversation back to honorable and useful areas of discourse such as virtue, self-discipline, and methods of acquiring useful information and attaining wisdom about the human condition and the various challenges to which it is typically subjected. Talk, for example, about which team is going to win the Super Bowl, can be left to wayward intellects with nothing more significant to discuss and no real concern for decency or honor. Leave the "bread and circuses" to the "common folk," and bend *your* efforts on improving *your own* character.

33-c. Don't allow your laughter be much, nor on many occasions, nor profuse. Avoid swearing, if possible, altogether; if not, as far as you are able. Avoid public and vulgar entertainments; but, if ever an occasion calls you to them, keep your attention upon the stretch, that you may not imperceptibly slide into vulgar manners. For be assured that if a person be ever so sound himself, yet, if his companion be infected, he who converses with him will be infected likewise.

Laughter is all well and good as long as it is a genuine good-natured expression of happiness and not a matter of mockery or derision. There *can be* too much laughter, as enjoyable as it typically is, and it can inhibit and stultify useful discourse. The audience for a talented stand-up comic will probably laugh a great deal and enjoy themselves, but it would not be healthy or edifying to spend *every* night going to comedy clubs and never reading a book or engaging in edifying conversation with admirable persons. Similarly, swearing and other language that is likely to provoke needless anger and conflict is generally unnecessary and unhelpful—tempting though it may be on some occasions. You will not make yourself wiser or better by cursing a blue streak and getting yourself and others emotionally worked up rather than engaging in calm rational speech or discourse. Most of what your culture refers to as "entertainment" is, in reality, nothing more than vulgar, adolescent escapism and the contemporary equivalent of "bread and circuses" to distract the masses and keep them occupied with trivialities. Unfortunately, these distractions work fairly effectively and most of the masses are inclined to embrace the distraction of "bread and circuses," as they seem to have very little by way of better ideas about how to spend their spare time. You do *not* ennoble or improve yourself by cheering and hooting along with tens of thousands of people at a football game or a popular music concert. If you spend a great deal of time with persons who love trivial diversions, you will become much as they are. Surely, you have both the capacity and the obligation to aim higher than *that*. It is unwise to spend time in the company of persons who do *not* share your higher and nobler aims.

33-d. Provide things relating to the body no further than mere use; as meat, drink, clothing, house, family. But strike off and reject everything relating to show and delicacy. As far as possible, before marriage, keep yourself pure from familiarities with women, and, if you indulge them, let it be lawfully. But don't therefore be troublesome and full of reproofs to those who use these liberties, nor frequently boast that you yourself don't.

Your body is a tool, or a set of tools, and your body must be kept in reasonably suitable repair if it is to last a good long while and prove useful to you at the most crucial moments. Since you carry your body with you everywhere that you go, it is probably advisable to do what you can to try and keep yourself in good physical condition on a consistent basis. Your body is, as far as you can tell, the only one that you get. Similarly, your home, your clothing, your food, and your furniture are more useful and more practically valuable to you and your family if they are kept in good condition, and if they are as simple and functional as can be managed. Do not pursue needlessly extravagant food or pointlessly expensive cars or furniture. What, after all, is the *good* of the lavishness? It is unwise to waste money purchasing and maintaining goods that are needlessly elaborate, ornate, or expensive. Manage your funds wisely so that you will have access to sufficient wherewithal if some emergency crops up or if a friend or family member is in need of your assistance. You are also better off, and your spouse and family are better off, if you refrain from sexual relations prior to marriage. Such extramarital relations often lead to unwanted pregnancies, sexually transmitted diseases, and emotional turmoil that are unhealthy conditions, and tend to beget conflict that is pointlessly damaging to all concerned. Conduct yourself in appropriate fashion where these matters are concerned, but do not hector those who live differently and do not allow yourself to become a scold. Let other people lead their own lives without offering them your unsolicited advice. Consider how *you* react to unsolicited advice and practice the Golden Rule—do *not* do to others the things that you do not want done to you.

33-e. If anyone tells you that such a person speaks ill of you, don't make excuses about what is said of you, but answer: "He does not know my other faults, else he would not have mentioned only these."

You are not obligated to respond to every criticism, every insult, and every remark that anyone might pass about you. In fact, you have no obligation to respond to *any* such commentary. Indeed, if you decided to respond to *everything* to which a rejoinder might be offered, then you would have little or no time for doing anything else of greater value—and almost *anything* else you may choose to do is likely to be of greater value. A bit of self-deprecating humor at your own expense will do you no more harm than did the original insult, and it also demonstrates a bit of humility and a rational adult's reaction to those who speak ill of you. Socrates is alleged to have said this kind of thing when someone called him a monster (he was notoriously ugly) and also when people had occasion to accuse him of evil deeds and pernicious motives. Saying something like, "If he only knew me a little better, then he would know that I am far, *far* worse than he could possibly realize," is a bit of gentle mockery of the practice of dishing out insults, and it also tends to be generally disarming to those who might wish to stoke, or to instigate, some form of conflict or other. This is also a useful de-escalation tactic for those occasions on which a belligerent person tries to goad you into some kind of needless confrontation or provoke you to violence. If someone casts aspersions upon your family name, for instance, then you always have the option of responding with something like, "Well, I have read that we are all descended from primates with small brains, and my family tree does not really branch much, so I think my family have actually done pretty well for a bunch of inbred apes." Of course, remember the all-purpose, "Thank you for your constructive criticism, I appreciate the input." It is difficult to follow that with more vitriol—though attempts may still be made. What is all of that *noise* to you? The dogs are free to keep barking as the caravan moves on, but you are *not* obligated to pay heed to their yapping.

33-f. It is not necessary for you to appear often at public spectacles; but if ever there is a proper occasion for you to be there, don't appear more solicitous for anyone than for yourself; that is, wish things to be only just as they are, and him only to conquer who is the conqueror, for thus you will meet with no hindrance. But abstain entirely from declamations and derision and violent emotions. And when you come away, don't discourse a great deal on what has passed, and what does not contribute to your own amendment. For it would appear by such discourse that you were immoderately struck with the show.

It is usually a good idea to avoid large crowds and particularly festive gatherings as much as is reasonable, as all sorts of trouble may erupt when a mob is formed, but if you *must* attend such an event due to, for example, a professional obligation, then do not try to be the center of attention, and never intrude upon any conversation or other interaction unless you are invited to participate. Do not impose your company upon other persons without just cause. If you find that you are surrounded by people who insist upon: wildly cheering, shouting, hooting, or otherwise making a spectacle of their presence at the event in question, then you should be prepared to part ways with any and all persons who behave in this crude and childish fashion. You have no obligation to root for one team as opposed to another, or to clamber onto someone's shoulders, or even to sing along with the band if you are at a concert. You need not applaud any performance that does not inspire *sincere* approbation to your way of thinking. Remember that *you* are *not* part of the show and that no one came to this event to watch *you*. After the event is over, you should avoid speaking at length about anything that occurred, because this will indicate to other people that you are impressed with something that happened, and you really should not indicate any particular interest in sports contests, musical performances, or other shows that are little more than silly amusements. Always remember that your overarching purpose is the development of wisdom and virtue. What has any amusement, contest, or concert got to do with that? You will never *win* virtue by playing *games*.

33-g. Go not [of your own accord] to the rehearsals of any authors, nor appear [at them] readily. But, if you do appear, keep your gravity and sedateness, and at the same time avoid being morose.

When it comes to attending plays, movies, other staged performances, or any production that is intended to elicit either laughter, tears, horror, or other explosive emotional responses, you should avoid these types of events, and these types of mental states, as much as possible. If you are *obligated* to attend, then you should do so only as part of some larger and more edifying project, and you should avoid getting caught up in needless emotional excitement. Perhaps you may attend a play, for example, because it elucidates an important facet of the human condition or it has some educational value beyond mere escapist amusement. Whatever the purpose of the event, and whatever the intentions of the authors, the actors, the musicians, or the other persons in attendance, you are always obligated to maintain proper decorum and, more importantly, maintain rationally guided indifference to the various emotions expressed within the production, elicited among others in the crowd, and especially those that might be expected on your part. What do you care for another person's expectations? There is no rational justification for allowing your psychological or emotional states to be dictated by elements of the production, or by the words and actions of those composing the audience. Nothing that happens on the stage or screen, and nothing that any member of the audience does or says, can ever causally determine your behavior, or compel you to adopt any particular frame of mind. All the weeping, wailing, and gnashing of teeth around you should not cause *you* to despair. Always remember that your moral and rational purpose is the attainment of wisdom and virtue, the constant improvement of your character, and setting a good example as an adult in command of yourself and your faculties. Your job is to be as upstanding as you are able. That job does not require you to join in with the mob or with any silly histrionics.

33-h. When you are going to confer with anyone, and particularly of those in a superior station, represent to yourself how Socrates or Zeno would behave in such a case, and you will not be at a loss to make a proper use of whatever may occur.

Identify the one or two persons, either currently alive or historical figures, whom you most admire, and then try to conduct yourself as if you are meeting with one of those persons any time that you face a conference in a business, political, or academic environment. Some Christians derive benefit from asking, "What would Jesus do?" and trying their best to conduct themselves in the manner that they believe that Jesus would have behaved. There is nothing wrong with this example, but if you are not Christian, or if you find it difficult to imagine getting your behavior to conform to a being that many regard as divine, then you can benefit from choosing a mere mortal, but a noble and admirable mortal, to emulate. It is important, however, that you choose your exemplar *very* carefully. A lot of philosophers, when Epictetus was teaching and also today, would choose Socrates as a hero to emulate. The Stoic philosophers were fairly uniformly impressed with the example of Socrates, the manner in which he lived his life, and especially the courageous comportment with which he faced his death. If you are reading this book, perhaps you might ask yourself how Epictetus would have handled the meeting for which you are preparing, or how one of the figures that Epictetus admired might have done so. Some people may find a greater affinity with the other great Roman Stoics, Marcus Aurelius and Seneca. There are, of course, lots of other examples of wise and noble people who are not associated with Stoicism or with philosophy. Perhaps you will derive inspiration from examples such as Moses, St. Francis, or Mohammed. There are plenty of historical exemplars from which to choose. Keep a hero in mind and try to behave in consistently gallant and noble fashion. Perhaps someone will emulate *your* example someday.

33-i. When you are going to any of the people in power, represent to yourself that you will not find him at home; that you will not be admitted; that the doors will not be opened to you; that he will take no notice of you. If, with all this, it is your duty to go, bear what happens, and never say [to yourself], "It was not worth so much." For this is vulgar, and like a man dazed by external things.

There are various forms that the Stoic "reserve clause" may take, and you are free to consider a host of possible contingencies that could disrupt your plans or prevent them from coming to fruition. If you are driving to a job interview, for example, then you might want to consider the possibility that you will get caught in traffic and end up being late, or the possibility that there will be a scheduling error and you will not even have the opportunity to attend the interview. These kinds of things happen, and there is not a great deal that you can do about external affairs. Should you have the opportunity to answer the interview questions, it may turn out that you do not quite answer as the selection committee prefers, or it may turn out that you are actually excluded from genuine consideration due to some immutable characteristic that does not appeal to the people making the selection. Perhaps, unbeknownst to you, the committee has been instructed to hire a candidate with characteristics that you simply lack. This kind of thing happens all the time, but it is rarely mentioned to the general public. Furthermore, it is always possible that, upon learning more about the job or about your potential coworkers and the job environment, you may realize that you either do not want the job any longer, or that you are not as well qualified as you had believed. These are only a handful of the *many* things that could come between you and the employment situation for which you had hoped. Also, a job interview is, obviously, only *one* of the innumerably many conditions crying out for the "reserve clause." Consider everything that could prevent your planned wedding day from going as expected. Potential hindrances beyond your control are simply *legion*.

33-j. In parties of conversation, avoid a frequent and excessive mention of your own actions and dangers. For, however agreeable it may be to yourself to mention the risks you have run, it is not equally agreeable to others to hear your adventures. Avoid, likewise, an endeavor to excite laughter. For this is a slippery point, which may throw you into vulgar manners, and, besides, may be apt to lessen you in the esteem of your acquaintance. Approaches to indecent discourse are likewise dangerous. Whenever, therefore, anything of this sort happens, if there be a proper opportunity, rebuke him who makes advances that way; or, at least, by silence and blushing and a forbidding look, show yourself to be displeased by such talk.

It is rarely advisable to talk a great deal about yourself and your accomplishments (real or imagined). Most people are far less interested in you and your exploits than you are likely to be if you have not made significant progress in the realm of self-rectification and the development of humility. Excessive discussion of *your* endeavors is almost always unbecoming and it bespeaks an unhealthy fixation upon selfish concerns and upon being the center of attention in any gathering or conversation. Not *everything* is about *you*. In fact, almost *nothing* is about you. It is advisable that you should also remember that there are many topics of conversation that nearly always lead to gossip, or to discreditable talk and behavior. Do not speak publicly about anything that is inherently private or about the sort of thing that is likely to stoke resentment, anger, or needless conflict. If one or more of your interlocutors is likely to perceive a question as prying into the personal realm, then it is advisable to avoid inquiries of that sort and stick to more worthy topics. Do not attempt to peer into another person's business in a manner that you would find objectionable were the roles reversed.

Although you should not broach inappropriate topics, it is not necessary for you to upbraid someone else who does so on the odd occasion. It is usually enough that *you* avoid participation in unsuitable talk. You are not required to act as a censor and you are not the Chief of the Speech Police either. Do not attempt to deprive other persons of their freedom of expression.

34. If you are struck by the appearance of any promised pleasure, guard yourself against being hurried away by it; but let the affair wait your leisure, and procure yourself some delay. Then bring to your mind both points of time: that in which you will enjoy the pleasure, and that in which you will repent and reproach yourself after you have enjoyed it; and set before you, in opposition to these, how you will be glad and applaud yourself if you abstain. And even though it should appear to you a seasonable gratification, take heed that its enticing, and agreeable and attractive force may not subdue you; but set in opposition to this how much better it is to be conscious of having gained so great a victory.

When a potentially desirable experience presents itself to your imagination, it is wise to first consider whether the satisfaction of this desire would be morally appropriate, or whether it is a prurient interest that has thrust itself into your mind. The advice, "If it feels good, do it!" is, arguably, the single most dangerous and ill-conceived bit of instruction ever to become a popular slogan. An adulterous affair that "feels good" in the sense that it is physically pleasurable is *not* an appropriate object of your desire, and you will degrade your character if you pursue it. Other desires may not be morally objectionable, but they may be unhealthy or unwise for other reasons. Do not, for example, eat and drink *everything* that appeals to your palate. Gluttony is, for good reasons, classed among the Seven Deadly Sins, and you will not derive pride or self-improvement from living a gluttonous self-indulgent life of physical dissolution. You will not flourish by turning yourself into, for example, an overweight alcoholic wreck. There is genuine, stable and deep satisfaction to be derived from mastering and extirpating your unhealthy and irrational tendencies. There is far greater satisfaction in marshaling the willpower to *quit* smoking than there is in taking yet another drag from a cigarette. Do the kinds of things that will enhance your body, mind, and character, and eschew the kinds of tendencies that lead in the opposite direction. You will find many, *many* ways to go wrong, and far fewer paths to virtue and decency.

35. When you do anything from a clear judgment that it ought to be done, never shun the being seen to do it, even though the world should make a wrong supposition about it; for, if you don't act right, shun the action itself; but, if you do, why are you afraid of those who censure you wrongly?

Doing the right thing is never a legitimate cause for shame; in fact, it should result in the opposite mental state, pride, and it makes no difference if others ridicule you or mock you for the behavior in question. Good and evil are *not* determined by a show of hands, and the popularity or commonality of a particular type of behavior is *not* evidence that it is morally appropriate or rationally justifiable. It is not terribly uncommon that a behavior is both morally praiseworthy and generally frowned upon nonetheless. Similarly, the fact that the masses approve of a particular form of behavior is hardly evidence that the behavior in question is virtuous or admirable. Consider the common sexual norms and mores of the contemporary world, and ask yourself if these are wise, healthy, or admirable. There are, of course, actions that you ought to avoid at all costs, but the justification for doing so is that the act in question is *inherently* immoral or irrational, and the attitude of the untutored masses is irrelevant to such determinations. Let your actions conform to nature, reason, and the moral law, and let those who criticize you for such behavior have their delusions as they wish. As for actions that do *not* conform to nature, reason, and the moral law, steer clear of this form of behavior, and steer clear of persons who engage in such acts as well as those who encourage you to do things that you know to be repugnant. You have nothing to fear from people who despise you or your behavior. All they can do is speak ill of you, and you know that their words and their beliefs have no purchase upon your decency. Let them call you whatever they wish, none of them can make their criticisms of you *true*, if you are, in fact, doing the right thing. Also, do not be persuaded by the mere praise of the masses. *Reason* must guide your behavior.

36. As the proposition, "Either it is day or it is night," is extremely proper for a disjunctive argument, but quite improper in a conjunctive one, so, at a feast, to choose the largest share is very suitable to the bodily appetite, but utterly inconsistent with the social spirit of an entertainment. When you eat with another, then, remember not only the value of those things which are set before you to the body, but the value of that behavior which ought to be observed towards the person who gives the entertainment.

What you crave and what is morally and rationally appropriate may not always be the same thing, and they may not be mutually compatible. If your cravings diverge from propriety or decency, then you are obligated to do the appropriate and decent thing, and to allow your inappropriate desire to go unsatisfied. It is also advisable that you inspect the *causes* of your inappropriate cravings and do your best to extirpate desires that can lead to unwise, unhealthy, or otherwise ignominious behavior. Should you be invited to a dinner party, and should the host serve one of your favorite dishes, then you may be tempted to indulge your appetite and take a second helping. As far as your body and your craving for your favorite food are concerned, this may seem quite reasonable, especially if you skipped lunch and are particularly hungry. As far as your host and the other guests are concerned, however, it is clear that this is not at all reasonable, because others at the dinner party may end up with none, or with a smaller portion than your host intended, and such matters are not appropriate for *you* to determine. You have no right to determine the dispensation of food or drink that is provided, prepared, and paid for by the host who was generous enough to invite you and the other guests to dinner. You are, therefore, obligated to restrain your appetite and take no more than your fair share of the meal. This is required by propriety, decorum, and rational self-discipline. Do not be the glutton who causes others to go unsatisfied. Surely, you ought to be a better guest than *that*. Behave in another person's home as you hope other persons would behave in *your* home.

37. If you have assumed any character above your strength, you have both made an ill figure in that and quitted one which you might have supported.

Do not pose as someone who is better, wiser, more knowledgeable, or more powerful and influential than you actually are. It is both unbecoming and dishonest to pretend that you are capable of accomplishing deeds that are, in fact, well beyond your abilities. If you are a law enforcement official and you *promise*, for example, that you will have a criminal brought to justice in an instance in which you lack the wherewithal to *guarantee* that the criminal will, in fact, be tried and convicted, then the victims, the families, and the public to whom you have issued your promise will be disappointed, the criminal will go free, and you will have revealed yourself to be a self-aggrandizing clown. It is entirely inappropriate for you to lay claim to powers and abilities that are, in reality, above or beyond your station and your actual capacities. Be honest with yourself and with others about what you do, and do not, have the power to accomplish. If it is within your ability to achieve some good deed, then by all means see to it that the deed is done and done properly. Make *no* promises, however, pertaining to conditions that are beyond your control. Given that you can, in the final analysis, control *nothing* beyond your own mental states and behaviors, then you should not issue guarantees that pertain to anything other than your own actions. So, you should feel free to promise that *you* will *not* commit any criminal act, but you should not guarantee an event that requires the participation of police, judges, juries, and other persons and things that you *cannot* control. You can promise to do everything *in your power* to bring some miscreant to justice, but you should not promise *success* in this endeavor. If you are a politician, you can make promises concerning only the vote that *you* will cast. You should *not* make promises that your vote will carry the day. Yours is nothing more than one vote among many. Govern your own character, and do not get upset about the behavior of those who govern the nation. They do not obey your commands.

38. When walking, you are careful not to step on a nail or turn your foot; so likewise be careful not to hurt the ruling faculty of your mind. And, if we were to guard against this in every action, we should undertake the action with the greater safety.

It is both wise and natural to protect your body, to take care of your health and physical well-being, and to avoid unnecessary dangers to life and limb. You look both ways before you cross the street because you have the perfectly reasonable desire to avoid getting crushed and killed by a moving vehicle. You pay attention because you do not want to be killed or injured. In the same way, you should pay attention to those things that endanger your mind, your reason, and your moral fiber, and you should be even more careful with these than you are with your body. Do you (so to speak) "look both ways" before making decisions about where you will direct your mental energies, and do you consider whether this expenditure of your time and energy is likely to be edifying or ennobling? If you fail to do so, then you place your mind and your decency needlessly at risk. Before you chose your career, did you consider only the salary and benefits associated with it, or did you also ask yourself if this type of job would prove fulfilling for you, or edifying for others, and did you consider the possibility that some occupations are more likely to require immoral behavior than are others, or that some occupations are far more stressful and psychologically unhealthy than are others? When you identify potential friends and associates, do you mostly rely on proximity and spend your time around people who just happen to work where you work or live in your neighborhood, or do you take the time to get a sense of the moral and intellectual qualities of the persons with whom you choose to spend your time? If you marry, do not choose a spouse who is merely attractive or wealthy, but choose one who will be a good parent and life partner. If your spouse is not trustworthy and honorable, then you should not expect your marriage to enhance your pursuit of a flourishing life. Indeed, marriage to a dishonorable spouse is a bit like stepping on a nail that is extremely difficult to pull out of your foot.

39. The body is to everyone the measure of the possessions proper for it, just as the foot is of the shoe. If, therefore, you stop at this, you will keep the measure; but if you move beyond it, you must necessarily be carried forward, as down a cliff; as in the case of a shoe, if you go beyond its fitness to the foot, it comes first to be gilded, then purple, and then studded with jewels. For to that which once exceeds a due measure, there is no bound.

It would be foolish and wasteful to purchase shoes that are far too large to fit your feet, or to buy footwear that are adorned in expensive ways that do not enhance the functionality of the shoe. They are likely to cost you more money than is necessary or sensible, they are probably going to be needlessly uncomfortable, and they are going to become damaged and useless to you in short order. Similarly, if you purchase clothes that fit well, but that are pointlessly elaborate, ornate, and ludicrously expensive, then you are wasting money that could be spent far more wisely and felicitously on necessities for you and your family. Your footwear and your other clothing are utterly inconsequential for anything other than practical purposes, and you behave foolishly if you concern yourself about impressing people with your shoes or your stylish clothing. This is only one example of a foolish concern, but the point is fairly clear. Do you waste time, money, energy, or concern on conditions that simply do not matter, and that have nothing to do with your moral fiber, or your intellectual advancement? This is foolishness. The same lesson applies to your home, your car, your furniture, and any other possessions you might wish to consider. There is no good reason to own more property, or to purchase exorbitantly expensive property, when you can make do with fewer things cluttering your life, and when you can waste far less money on simpler possessions. If you waste money on things that you do not need, then you risk having insufficient funds for things that really matter to the well-being of your family and friends. A noble member of the family does not place the family at risk without very good reasons.

40. Women from fourteen years old are flattered with the title of "mistresses" by the men. Therefore, perceiving that they are regarded only as qualified to give the men pleasure, they begin to adorn themselves, and in that to place ill their hopes. We should, therefore, fix our attention on making them sensible that they are valued for the appearance of decent, modest and discreet behavior.

It is unwise and immoral to treat young women as if they are only valuable insofar as they are attractive to men or useful for sexual purposes. Do not mistreat young women, and do not disgrace and degrade yourself by acting as a letch or a pederast who fails to note the humanity of girls and women. If girls and young women are presented with this type of treatment repeatedly, then they are likely to focus their energies on trying to make themselves appear pleasing to men, and they are likely to neglect the proper development of their character, intellect, and virtue. The last thing that any culture should do with regard to its girls and young women is to encourage them to believe that their only viable options are marrying well or perhaps even becoming prostitutes. Neither of these goals is admirable for young ladies and both options are unworthy of pursuit by *virtuous* women. A *good* society should encourage girls and young women to develop the virtues of the mind, the character, and appropriate interpersonal relations. A *morally good* society should want to produce *morally good* women (and men). Young women and young men should be taught modesty, propriety, discretion, and decency in their dealings with each other and with their elders. If society teaches young people that they are only valued for their attractiveness or for pleasures of the flesh, then that society is going to produce a depraved culture of sexual obsession that is devoid of interest in accumulating wisdom, virtue, and understanding the natural world or as yet undiscovered elements of the human condition. There is much more to life than sex, and a culture sows the seeds of its own destruction when it indulges in and encourages sexual obsession. It is far better to encourage fascination with loftier and nobler concerns.

41. It is a mark of want of genius to spend much time in things relating to the body, as to be long in our exercises, in eating and drinking, and in the discharge of other animal functions. These should be done incidentally and slightly, and our whole attention be engaged in the care of the understanding.

As your overarching goal is the attainment of wisdom and the improvement of your character, it is counterproductive to spend too much time and energy concerned with the appearance of your body, or obsessing about the food and drink that enters your body and, later, leaves your body. Keep in mind that you really only *borrow* food and drink from the surrounding world. It is, of course, necessary to take in nutrients to sustain the body and its proper functioning, and it is useful to keep your body healthy enough to function in accordance with virtues such as courage and temperance. Since martial courage is useless without a properly functioning body that is in condition to engage in the protection or defense of yourself, or your family, or your community, or innocents in your charge, it is advisable to train your body for functionality in martial or combative skills. It is irresponsible to allow your body to fall into disrepair before its natural time. Beyond these types of considerations, however, it is irrational to devote too much time, effort, and energy to activities such as weightlifting, obsessive dieting, or the type of attention to your appearance that is common among professional models. Keep the most important tools in good operating condition, and recognize that your body is one set of essential tools for accomplishing tasks that are appropriate to your role within the family, the community, and your occupation. Beyond the necessary upkeep, excessive concern with your appearance is, at least arguably, a form of narcissism, and it betrays unhealthy values, and principles of conduct that depart from virtuous behavior. You are not, after all, training to compete in bodybuilding competition, are you? You are not a model, are you? Do not behave as if you are. Do not primp, preen, and pose when you ought to be working on the health of your body, mind, and character.

42. When any person harms you, or speaks badly of you, remember that he acts or speaks from a supposition of its being his duty. Now, it is not possible that he should follow what appears right to you, but what appears so to himself. Therefore, if he judges from a wrong appearance, he is the person hurt, since he too is the person deceived. For if anyone should suppose a true proposition to be false, the proposition is not hurt, but he who is deceived about it. Setting out, then, from these principles, you will meekly bear a person who reviles you, for you will say upon every occasion, "It seemed so to him."

People make all sorts of decisions and engage in all sorts of behaviors, and it is not worth the time and effort required to try to discern their motives in all of the various circumstances that you, and they, may encounter. Furthermore, you can never be certain about another person's intentions, or about the life events that might have contributed to the worldview and value system that influence the intentions underlying the actions that you may observe. If a person of your acquaintance makes a decision that you believe to be unwise or inappropriate, then it is important to remember that this person chooses in accordance with his beliefs, his values, and his experience, and these may all be very different from your beliefs, values, and experience. If this person has false beliefs or indecent values, then *he* is the one who will suffer the damage to his character, and *he* is the one who will behave in a manner that is not conducive to success or self-improvement. None of that is properly *your* concern, as you have not been empowered to govern your friend's life, but only your *own*. Do not become angry with a person who is simply confused, misinformed, or acting in accordance with a faulty set of principles. If this person criticizes *you* on the basis of a misperception, a set of false beliefs, or some faulty values, then *you* are *not* harmed by his false judgment, and you need not take the criticism to heart. What other people believe about you is, in the final analysis, none of your business. Do you believe that other people are entitled to know *all* of your thoughts? If not, then do not behave as if you are entitled to know *their* thoughts, and do not insist upon them regarding you in one fashion as opposed to another.

43. **Everything has two handles, the one by which it may be carried, the other by which it cannot. If your brother acts unjustly, don't lay hold on the action by the handle of his injustice, for by that it cannot be carried; but by the opposite, that he is your brother, that he was brought up with you; and thus you will lay hold on it, as it is to be carried.**

With respect to any event and any person's behavior, the option of how you want to handle the person and the event in question is always open to several alternative responses, and you always have more than one way to approach the situation in question. Suppose your parents die, as is not terribly unlikely to happen at some point or other, and suppose further that your siblings respond to their deaths in a manner that you initially regard as greedy or selfish. Will *you* benefit, will you *ennoble* yourself, will you *improve* the circumstances that matter, if you become outraged by this perceived misbehavior and respond to your brother or sister as if you have been attacked? Surely, *you* cannot be harmed by their greed or selfishness. How will an angry response to your brother's behavior or your sister's behavior enhance your relationship with your family? How will responding to greed with outrage cause you to become a better person, or help your siblings in any way? Clearly, there is no benefit to your character that will derive from a needless conflict with one or more members of your own family. Obviously, the family as a unit will not be better off or healthier as a result of some internecine squabble over money or property. It is shameful to engage in this type of conflict within your own family. Do you not value your integrity and your decency more than you value some amount of money, or a house, or some collection of trinkets? If you are not willing to sacrifice the material "goods" for the sake of maintaining harmony and good relations within your own family, then it may well be that *you* are the real problem. Do not accuse your own family of greed while fighting with them over money. This makes you a hypocrite as well as a terrible sibling. Surely, you cannot believe that it is either wise or noble to value money or material things more than you value your family and good relations among your nearest and dearest.

44. These reasonings are unconnected: "I am richer than you, therefore I am better"; "I am more eloquent than you, therefore I am better." The connection is rather this: "I am richer than you, therefore my property is greater than yours;" "I am more eloquent than you, therefore my style is better than yours." But you, after all, are neither property nor style.

A wealthy miscreant is not superior to a pauper who conducts himself in a dignified fashion and pursues virtue. Diogenes the Cynic, for example, owned virtually nothing, but this gives us no information about his character, his wisdom, or his fortitude. All the money in the world does not have the power to make a fool into a wise man, nor can it turn an indecent human being into a moral exemplar. It is not uncommon for wealthy persons to believe themselves to be superior to others on account of their riches, nor is it particularly uncommon for the masses to treat wealthy persons as if they are superior to others on account of the wealth that they have amassed. This is, of course, a mistake. Billionaires have more money than you have (presumably), but they are not, by virtue of their riches, morally or intellectually superior to you merely because they can purchase expensive products that you cannot afford, or because they travel around the world at their whim. Go where they may, lousy human beings remain lousy human beings. What is the magic in an expensive automobile that imparts wisdom and virtue to its possessor? Where is the room in a mansion that turns a repugnant human being into a saint upon his entry into it? Of course, no such things occur in reality. If your home costs you more money than mine, and if we both get roughly the same protection from the elements out of our respective domiciles, then what is your alleged advantage? Perhaps your neighborhood is less saturated with violent criminals than is mine. This may well be an advantage of sorts, but it is clearly not the type of advantage that makes you *morally superior* to me. If you wish to be morally upstanding, then you take a circuitous route to virtue via the mansion and the fancy car. No limousine will take you to your destination if the place you seek is to be found *within* you and if that place can only be approached in *humility*.

45. Does anyone bathe in a mighty little time? Don't say that he does it ill, but in a mighty little time. Does anyone drink a great quantity of wine? Don't say that he does ill, but that he drinks a great quantity. For, unless you perfectly understand the principle from which anyone acts, how should you know if he acts ill? Thus you will not run the hazard of assenting to any appearances but such as you fully comprehend.

Do not presume that you know why other people are doing what they are doing or why they are doing what they are doing *in the way* that they are doing it. In other words, do not judge another person's actions, methods, or motives. If you should notice that a guest in your home drinks an enormous amount of wine or spirits then all you can conclude safely is that your guest is drinking more than the average person drinks in the same amount of time. No other judgment follows from your observations. It would be inappropriate to leap to the conclusion that your guest is an alcoholic or that he is trying to "drown his sorrows" with drink. Indeed, it would be inappropriate to conclude that your guest is drinking "too much," because you do not know what his purposes are or what he intends to accomplish by drinking this much alcohol. Perhaps your guest has made arrangements for someone else to drive home, and perhaps he is fascinated with the flavor of the wine you are serving, and perhaps he has a tremendous tolerance for alcohol and, therefore, he has no concern about becoming sick or behaving badly due to the influence of the wine. It is not rationally justifiable to draw conclusions that are not supported by the available evidence or by the mere "appearances" as they present themselves to your senses. If you do not know another person's intentions, and it is impossible to know them with *certainty*, then you have no business attributing to that other person any impropriety or flawed behavior. How many times, after all, have *your* intentions been misunderstood? It is wise to be circumspect when you attribute character traits, especially character *defects*, to persons other than yourself. Surely, you have enough of your own peccadilloes to warrant the devotion of all of your spare time and energy to rectifying *those*, rather than worrying about everyone else and about flaws you imagine *they* may have.

46-a. Never call yourself a philosopher, nor talk a great deal among the unlearned about theorems, but act conformably to them. Thus, at an entertainment, don't talk how persons ought to eat, but eat as you ought. For remember that in this manner Socrates also universally avoided all ostentation. And when persons came to him and desired to be recommended by him to philosophers, he took and recommended them, so well did he bear being overlooked.

It is far more important to live the life of a wise and honorable person than it is to be able to discourse *about* the topic or to *describe* yourself, or someone else, as wise and honorable. Anyone, after all, can *call herself* anything, and anyone can *attribute to himself* any properties that his imagination may conjure. Doing so does not make the attributions *true*, and does not improve anyone's character. The manner in which you *conduct* yourself reveals your true character and not the manner in which you talk about yourself or the manner in which others talk about you. Watching reveals more than listening in this arena. Heroic figures from the history of philosophy, politics, and religion have successfully avoided self-aggrandizement, and they are widely admired for their modesty and self-discipline. Socrates, Epictetus, Marcus Aurelius, Jesus, St. Francis, Gandhi, Mother Teresa, and Nelson Mandela have all advocated simplicity of values, and humility of character. Some have managed to do so and, more importantly, managed to conduct themselves in accordance with their stated values, to "practice what they preached," in extremely disadvantageous circumstances. Nonetheless, all of these modest, humble men and women managed to exert tremendous cultural influence and exhort their fellow human beings to lives of virtue and decency. So, if you find that you are disregarded or overlooked by anyone then you should remind yourself that many good, decent, and honorable people have been treated in similar fashion—indeed, many good, decent, and honorable people have been treated far worse than you can readily imagine. This did not prevent them from living praiseworthy, admirable lives. Do not allow anything to prevent *you* from living well either.

46-b. So that if ever any talk should happen among the unlearned concerning philosophic theorems, be you, for the most part, silent. For there is great danger in immediately throwing out what you have not digested. And, if anyone tells you that you know nothing, and you are not nettled at it, then you may be sure that you have begun your business.

There is, for the most part, no good reason to go out of your way to demonstrate to other persons that you are learned and erudite. Needless displays of intellectual or rhetorical prowess are indicative of insecurity, and they also tend to alienate the very audience with whom you are attempting to communicate. Thus, such displays are counterproductive to your purposes, unless your only real purpose is to show off for the crowd. Showing off is not a noble aim, and it behooves you to avoid this type of adolescent display. Furthermore, you ought to take care that you understand the context in which any conversation is taking place, including the level of understanding attained or exhibited by the various participants concerning the subject of discussion, before you decide to participate and offer your "two cents" regarding the matter. Even if you *are* more knowledgeable in a particular subject area than the others who are speaking, it does not necessarily follow that your input will be welcome, or that you are entitled to chime in. Perhaps you have happened upon a private conversation among people who do not know you and are not interested in your opinion or your experience with the topic of discussion. Maybe *no one cares* what you have to say about the matter. If your effort to join in the conversation is rebuffed and rebuked, then you would probably do well to simply stop talking, walk away, and waste no further time or thought regarding the interaction. After all, no one is *obligated* to welcome your company or your utterances. Remember that freedom of association entails freedom *from* association, and not everyone wants you around. You have heard, have you not, that you should not stay where you are not wanted? That is good advice. Do not make a nuisance or a burden of yourself if you can help it.

46-c. For sheep don't throw up the grass to show the shepherds how much they have eaten; but, inwardly digesting their food, they outwardly produce wool and milk. Thus, therefore, do you likewise not show theorems to the unlearned, but the actions produced by them after they have been digested.

Just as animals do not eat for the purpose of vomiting and demonstrating their capacity to eat a great deal, and then show it to the world, so should you recognize that the purpose of learning is *not* spouting rhetorical flourishes or quoting learned philosophers, historians, and scientists. The purpose of learning and acquiring wisdom is the *living* of a noble, honorable, decent, and otherwise virtuous *life*. Are you more interested in *appearing* to be wise, particularly to those who are *unwise*, or are you primarily interested in accumulating genuine wisdom and deploying your learning to construct an admirable and honorable character for yourself, as well as a rationally defensible set of values that will guide you through a flourishing life of decency, serenity, and temperance? If your interest is the former, then you are no better than a show pony that has been trained to care only for applause and accolades, but is unconcerned about genuine health, well-being, and functionality. Do not turn yourself into the human equivalent of a vain show pony that lives as if you have been trained only for making a pleasant appearance to the masses. Socrates was notoriously ugly, but remained untroubled about his appearance because his goals were loftier than winning a beauty contest. Marcus Aurelius was notoriously humble, even though he was the last competent Emperor of the Roman Empire, as well as the most politically and militarily powerful human being on the planet. He understood that real conquests do not occur on battlefields littered with the dead, but that true greatness is the conquest of one's own *ego*. Diogenes the Cynic was notoriously poor and homeless, apart from a wine barrel, but his example of austerity and independence still inspires people today. These lives were *not* lived for show. These lives were dedicated to the pursuit of heights to which most people dare not attain. Do you want your life to be something common, or do you want your life to constitute a noble journey? This question really should not be terribly difficult to answer.

47. When you have brought yourself to supply the necessities of your body at a small price, don't pique yourself upon it; nor, if you drink water, be saying upon every occasion, "I drink water." But first consider how much more sparing and patient of hardship the poor are than we. But if at any time you would inure yourself by exercise to labor, and bearing hard trials, do it for your own sake, and not for the world; don't grasp statues, but, when you are violently thirsty, take a little cold water in your mouth, and spurt it out and tell nobody.

It is both unbecoming and entirely unnecessary for you to make a show of your efforts, your practice, and of any suffering you may endure in the process of trying to make yourself into a better and wiser person. If you consider the plight of those who live in poverty, those who endure oppression, and those who have had to face challenges that you can barely imagine, then you will recognize that you have no justification to enjoy and to take pride in your meager accomplishments, and you have incontrovertible justification for the experience of tremendous and unwavering gratitude for the many unearned benefits that you enjoy. Do not brag, even in the confines of your own consciousness, about any progress that you might make, and always recognize the advantages you have enjoyed due to fate and happenstance. How many people, historically, have had access to all of the benefits that you so often take for granted? Consider the plight of the ancients. What would you have accomplished had you been given *their* circumstances? So, if you should endure some minor hardship without complaint, then you do so only, at least in part, by virtue of your willpower, and you do so, in large part, by virtue of conditions with which you have been gifted through no special effort on your part. For that reason, and also because you do not ennoble your character through efforts to impress other people, you really ought to avoid making a show of your practices, your alleged progress, or your austerities. It is more than enough that you simply *do* the right thing. You need not inform others of your alleged righteousness. Tall people, after all, do not need to *tell* anyone how tall they are. If your virtues are not apparent to anyone who might be paying attention to your conduct, then you may begin to wonder how the others fail to perceive your "obvious" merits, or you may have cause to consider the possibility that your alleged virtues are not quite so obvious because they are, in fact, illusory. How confident are you?

48-a. The condition and characteristic of a vulgar person, is, that he never expects either benefit or hurt from himself, but from externals. The condition and characteristic of a philosopher is, that he expects all hurt and benefit from himself. The marks of a proficient are, that he censures no one, praises no one, blames no one, accuses no one, says nothing concerning himself as being anybody, or knowing anything: when he is, in any instance, hindered or restrained, he accuses himself; and, if he is praised, he secretly laughs at the person who praises him; and, if he is censured, he makes no defense.

Most people look to external states of affairs to determine whether something good or bad has happened, and these people also attach their hopes and aspirations to events over which they have no control. They watch the stock market, they observe political conditions, and they pay attention to warfare and potential conflict across the globe, and they do this in an effort to find "good news" and "bad news." They proceed to respond to the news as if the external world is the primary condition determining their well-being. If you seek to become wise and virtuous, then you should recognize that none of the aforementioned states of affairs in any way contributes to your character or to how virtuous you may be. If the Dow Jones Industrial Average reaches a new high, you should know that such an eventuality does *not* endow *you* with courage, temperance, justice, or wisdom. If you despair because your 401k loses value, then you have made very little progress toward the realization that your wealth is not constitutive of your *decency*. You have no business complaining about what anyone else does or says, you have no business celebrating because of anything that you see or hear on the news, and you certainly have no business bragging to anyone, including yourself, about your alleged accomplishments and successes. The only conditions that truly matter are the conditions of your *character* and of your *moral* development. Improve *yourself* and do not fret about externals. There is, after all, no benefit to allowing yourself to get worked up about all of the things that you cannot control.

48-b. But he goes about with the caution of sick or injured people, dreading to move anything that is set right, before it is perfectly fixed. He suppresses all desire in himself; he transfers his aversion to those things only which thwart the proper use of our own faculty of choice; the exertion of his active powers towards anything is very gentle; if he appears stupid or ignorant, he does not care, and, in a word, he watches himself as an enemy, and one in ambush.

If you wish to become wise and virtuous, then you *must* recognize that nothing outside of your own mind and nothing other than *your failures* of proper self-discipline can prevent you from attaining those goals. You must learn to watch your own tendencies of thought and behavior, and you must train yourself to remain untroubled about what anyone else may think about you or say about you. Governing yourself in rational fashion is always within *your* control, therefore, you cannot justifiably blame anyone or anything else if you should fail to behave in an honorable fashion or if you should allow yourself to fall into any form of irrationality. Always remember not to blame anyone *else* if you are dissatisfied. When you allow yourself to desire any condition to appear in the external world, you thereby invite frustration should that condition fail to manifest. If, on the other hand, your desires and aversions attach *only* to conditions of your *own* character and behavior, then what could possibly prevent the satisfaction of your desires, and the avoidance of your aversions, apart from irrationality or indiscipline on *your* part? Do you wish to avoid the condition of being a liar? Do not lie. Thus, you will not incur that aversion. Do you wish to be a faithful spouse? Set your will to remaining faithful and never indulge in adultery. Thus, your desire will be satisfied. Do you wish for fame? Thus, you are a fool. Fame is a weak condition because it can be stripped from you by the disregard of the fickle public at any time. Fame does not make you a better or wiser person, and you should have no need of it. Do not become dependent in this way.

49-a. When anyone shows himself overly confident in ability to understand and interpret the works of Chrysippus, say to yourself, "Unless Chrysippus had written obscurely, this person would have had no subject for his vanity. But what do I desire? To understand nature and follow her. I ask, then, who interprets her, and, finding Chrysippus does, I have recourse to him. I don't understand his writings. I seek, therefore, one to interpret them."

People who like to show off their command of works written by intellectual luminaries do *not* demonstrate their own intellectual prowess by quoting some philosopher or literary figure or by producing a pretentious interpretation of an important work of genius. A lot of people can quote *Hamlet* and reveal its subtleties to the rest of us because they have spent a number of years in graduate school. None of those people, by virtue of these efforts or the classes they have taken, demonstrate that they are the intellectual or literary equivalent of Shakespeare. If you want to learn what virtue is, how to attain wisdom, and how to develop self-discipline, then there are many good sources from which to learn. Epictetus is one such source. Marcus Aurelius is another. Reading everything that Epictetus ever said, and reading all the commentaries on Epictetus will not, by itself, endow you with reason, wisdom, and virtue. The works of Epictetus, Seneca, Marcus Aurelius, Plato, Aristotle, Shakespeare, and *many* others are excellent sources, but you must both understand their works properly *and* put those works into practice throughout the course of living your life if you want to *embody* wisdom and virtue. So, you must decide whether you merely want to *appear* to be a good person, or *appear* to understand the works of good and wise persons, or whether you actually want to *be* a good and wise person. Nearly anyone can "talk a good game" about their accomplishments. Just about anyone can list a few of the cardinal virtues and say a few words about each of them. It takes a *genuinely* wise and decent human being to *embody* both sagacity and virtue. It is one thing to *talk* about a good life and something else entirely to *live* one.

49-b. So far there is nothing to value myself upon. And when I find an interpreter, what remains is to make use of his instructions. This alone is the valuable thing. But, if I admire nothing but merely the interpretation, what do I become more than a grammarian instead of a philosopher? Except, indeed, that instead of Homer I interpret Chrysippus. When anyone, therefore, desires me to read Chrysippus to him, I rather blush when I cannot show my actions agreeable and consonant to his discourse.

The only real value of studying philosophy, science, literature, or any other discipline is to be found in the practical application of the knowledge that you acquire through your studies. There is nothing inherently wrong with or defective about knowledge for its own sake, but if you do not use your acquired knowledge for some purpose, then it remains inert within you. You have declined to give it *life*. If you fail to put your understanding of these various disciplines into practice, then you are really nothing more than a person who reads *potentially* valuable works. There is something sad about wasted potential, is there not? Consider all that the world would have lost had Michelangelo studied the works of other artists, but had done nothing further with his studies. Imagine a world in which Isaac Newton read a great deal about mathematics, physics, and various studies of the natural world, but then he pursued a career as a baker or a cobbler. How long would the rest of us have waited for the scientific and intellectual advancements that flowed from Newton's work if he had not put his learning into practice. So, you can read anything you like, and you can spend your entire adult life studying the most important and influential works ever written, but if you do not *use* the information to transform your character and develop a more virtuous style of life, then your years of reading, studying, and education come to nothing of any great value. Your work of art *is* your life. Make it as beautiful and meaningful as you can manage. Become the best artist that you can. Show the world your life, your work of art, and let them make of it what they will.

50-a. Whatever moral rules you have deliberately proposed to yourself, abide by them as they were laws, and as if you would be guilty of impiety by violating any of them. Don't regard what anyone says of you, for this, after all, is no concern of yours. How long, then, will you put off thinking yourself worthy of the highest improvements and follow the distinctions of reason?

If you adopt a set of values and you derive principles by which to live in accordance with those core values, then you do not really embrace those values, and you do not really believe in those principles unless you live a life that *adheres* to them. You ought to treat every rule that you adopt to guide your conduct as an inviolable decree, and you would do well to imagine that God is watching (whether you believe in God or not) and judging your behavior. Even if you can fool your fellow human beings, you are told that God infallibly metes out justice. Perhaps this is so. What do you lose by acting as if God is watching? In this way, you will not become lax about your conduct or allow yourself to lapse into behavior of which a good God will disapprove (and issue punishment). In other words, conduct yourself as if your *eternal soul* is on the line (and you need not believe that you *literally have* an eternal soul in order to follow this rule). If you allow yourself to think that a lapse in honorable comportment is permissible on this or that occasion, then you engender a bad habit and you increase the likelihood that you will eventually become entirely dissolute. You cannot take your values and principles very seriously if you allow yourself to violate them periodically and you do not chastise yourself for these failures. You will, of course, fail on many occasions, but if you fail due to disinterest in success and decency, or due to a casual and flippant attitude about your moral and intellectual commitments, then you have failed indeed. If people make fun of you and your commitments, then you should be utterly indifferent to what they say about you. Your only proper concern is living a good life. Do not insist on applause for doing so. The masses, the common folk, do not generally appreciate virtue or burst into spontaneous celebration of wisdom. So much the worse, it would seem, for the teeming masses.

50-b. You have received the philosophical theorems, with which you ought to be familiar, and you have been familiar with them. What other master, then, do you wait for, to throw upon that the delay of reforming yourself? You are no longer a boy, but a grown man. If, therefore, you will be negligent and slothful, and always add procrastination to procrastination, purpose to purpose, and fix day after day in which you will attend to yourself, you will insensibly continue without proficiency, and, living and dying, persevere in being one of the vulgar.

The time is *now*, tomorrow is promised to no one, and you have no idea how much time remains in your life on this planet. Do not postpone your efforts to improve yourself. If you claim that you are committed to living a noble and honorable life, then you have no excuse for doing anything other than living that life *right now*. When you were a child, you thought and behaved in childish fashion. There is no shame in this. Children are permitted to be careless and silly. If, however, you continue to conduct yourself as if you are a child well into your adulthood, then you are still the moral and intellectual equivalent of a child, and you are merely hiding within the body of an adult. You cannot claim, with sincerity, to be concerned about moral decency and living a virtuous life if you decline to do so in *this moment*. When else were you planning to get to work? It is a bit like a person who claims to be utterly committed to losing weight but does not consume less, exercise more, or behave in any other way that might contribute to weight loss. Why would anyone take this alleged "commitment" seriously? If you say that you want to become a wiser and morally better person than you are today, then you *must* diligently address your efforts and your energy to putting the lessons you have learned into the *practice* of living a virtuous life. Anyone who fails to behave in a virtuous fashion ought to refrain from claiming to have any genuine interest in living a virtuous life. In this area, as well in many others, it is fairly easy to "talk the talk" but not nearly so easy to "walk the walk." Words are well and good, but virtue lives in *action*. Believe your eyes rather than your ears in such matters.

50-c. This instant, then, think yourself worthy of living as a man grown up, and a proficient. Let whatever appears to be the best be to you an inviolable law. And if any instance of pain or pleasure, or glory or disgrace, is set before you, remember that now is the combat, now the Olympiad comes on, nor can it be put off. By once being defeated and giving way, proficiency is lost, or by the contrary preserved. Thus Socrates became perfect, improving himself by everything, attending to nothing but reason. And though you are not yet a Socrates, you ought, however, to live as one desirous of becoming a Socrates.

You will meet with difficulties, challenges, and obstacles in your efforts to improve yourself and in your endeavors to become wise and virtuous. These obstacles are not rare, rather they are ubiquitous and they seem to multiply relentlessly. If you give up your quest because of these impediments, then you are as far away from your goal as if you had never taken up the quest at all. Socrates never allowed himself to be concerned with anything apart from actively using reason to pursue wisdom irrespective of any potential consequences of that pursuit, including his *death*. Socrates was the first philosopher, as far as we know, who was presented with the choice to either desist in his pursuit of wisdom, his practice of philosophy, or face execution. Socrates refused to debase himself by becoming an impious coward, and he chose to continue to "man the post" to which he claimed to have been assigned by the god Apollo, and he, therefore, chose to subject himself to execution rather than subjecting himself to moral degradation. That is genuine courage and dedication put into practice, and Socrates' death is an undeniable example of commitment to living a life of reason and virtue no matter what the risks and consequences. If Socrates can give his very life to the pursuit to virtue, then what excuse can *you* have for your *lack* of commitment to living in accordance with reason and pursuing virtue to the very best of your abilities? You are probably no Socrates, but his example in this matter is worthy of your emulation. Give it your best effort.

51-a. The first and most necessary topic in philosophy is that of the use of moral theorems, such as, "We ought not to lie;" the second is that of demonstrations, such as, "What is the origin of our obligation not to lie;" the third gives strength and articulation to the other two, such as, "What is the origin of this as a demonstration." For what is demonstration? What is consequence? What contradiction? What truth? What falsehood?

If you are going to pursue wisdom, virtue, and a well-lived life, then it will be necessary for you to master the principles of logic and reasoning so that you can critically evaluate information, evidence, and argument as they relate to the nature of your goals. Reasoning carefully and critically is indispensable to the goal of learning the deepest and most valuable lessons about the human condition. People who fail to develop their critical thinking skills are unlikely to make much progress in applying their rational faculty to the many claims they will encounter about the nature of good and evil, or about what it means to live life in an honorable fashion. In order to understand a rule of conduct, and internalize it so as to put the rule into practice, it is necessary to apprehend what the rule means, what evidence can be presented in support of the rule, and also how to go about distinguishing between compelling evidence and fallacious reasoning. If you do not know how to tell a true proposition from a false one, or if you cannot tell the difference between a good argument and a flawed one, then you are very likely to become confounded by the many different schools of thought concerning morality and the nature of the well-lived, flourishing life. You probably agree, for example, that murder is evil, but have you thought carefully about precisely what it is that *makes* murder evil, or about what sorts of evidence can be marshaled in order to convince someone who *denies* that it is evil, or someone who is undecided or uninterested? Consider trying to impart good values to children without being able to respond to their questions about the topic. The prospect of success in that endeavor is not enhanced by ignorance about morality.

51-b. The third topic, then, is necessary on the account of the second, and the second on the account of the first. But the most necessary, and that whereon we ought to rest, is the first. But we act just on the contrary. For we spend all our time on the third topic, and employ all our diligence about that, and entirely neglect the first. Therefore, at the same time that we lie, we are immediately prepared to show how it is demonstrated that lying is not right.

Unfortunately, many of those who are allegedly learned in the study of morality and propriety seem to devote all of their time and energy to producing complex arguments and justifications for moral principles that they neglect entirely in the conduct of their actual lives. There are many professional ethicists who have written entire books about ethical theory and the various applications of ethical theory to specific issues, who nonetheless conduct themselves in utterly unscrupulous fashion and never make even the slightest effort to improve their own character or modify their behavior. Consider the philosophers who extol the benefits of Stoic ethics, but who are also very concerned about how many books they sell, what royalty agreements they make with the publisher, and how many people watch and hear the interviews in which they are so desperate to appear clever and erudite. The number of "professional" Stoics seems to be on the increase. Socrates, Epictetus, and Marcus Aurelius did *not* lust after money, fame, and fans, nor did they seek to impress everyone they encountered with their intellectual prowess or their rhetorical skills. They devoted themselves, first and foremost, to living honorable lives in accordance with reason and virtue. If they became famous as a by-product of their endeavors, then they regarded fame as neither a great benefit nor a great detriment to their overarching purpose. It is not at all clear how many contemporary philosophers or other academics can honestly make the same assertion. The truly wise do not strive for accolades. If you wish to be honest and decent, then the attainment of those virtues will have to be reward enough.

52-a. Upon all occasions we ought to have these maxims ready at hand:

"Conduct me, Jove, and you, O Destiny,
Wherever your decrees have fixed my station."
– Cleanthes

It is advisable to keep pithy maxims at the ready so that you may recur to them at moments of trial or difficulty when duress makes a long treatise impossible to recall. You should not expect yourself to be able to memorize the complete works of Seneca, Epictetus, and Marcus Aurelius "chapter and verse," as it were, nor would that be a particularly efficient use of your limited time, energy, and memory. Luckily, there is no need to undertake such a daunting and complex project as that. The heart of Stoic philosophy, or much of the most important elements of it in any event, can be encapsulated fairly effectively as a comparative handful of rules that you may commit to memory much more readily than you could manage with hundreds of pages of text. Just as one need not memorize the entire *Bible* in order to recall and obey the *Ten Commandments*, similarly you do not have to memorize the full *Discourses of Epictetus* in order to adhere to the wisdom of Epictetus. Indeed, this *Handbook* (*Enchiridion*) was produced as an attempt to gather and organize the most important lessons from the larger collection of Epictetus' teaching. The reminder that "Destiny" will take you where you are going, and that it is both foolish and counterproductive to complain about your journey or your destination is captured in this bit of wisdom that Epictetus culled from the work of the earlier Stoic philosopher, Cleanthes. If you find that you are dissatisfied with the current state of affairs, then remind yourself that you are not in charge of the world, that you did not earn your place in it, that there could have been innumerably many worlds in which you made no appearance whatsoever, and that gratitude for your life is preferable to sustained bitterness. Consider all of the advantages and opportunities that you have, and that you did not earn, and try to muster commensurate gratitude.

52-b. "I follow cheerfully; and, did I not,
Wicked and wretched, I must follow still
Whoever yields properly to Fate, is deemed
Wise among men, and knows the laws of heaven."
– Euripides, Frag. 965

Like the Stoic image of the dog that is leashed to the moving cart and bound to follow it whether the dog consents or not, this reminder is useful when you find that events are not unfolding as you expected or perhaps as you might have preferred prior to careful reflection about your small part in the grand scheme of things. You can complain about the way of things and gripe about the circumstances in which you find yourself, but all the whining and moaning you may produce shall do *nothing* to improve your circumstances, and grumbling betrays a petulant rejection of reality as it stands. Who are *you* to say how the world "should be" or to become a malignant wretch that troubles yourself and others about the allegedly terrible state of things? The world unfolds as forces that are well beyond your power cause it to unfold, and all the discontent that you can muster will not alter the nature of the world or the behavior of the people in it. The world will always have its way with you, and resistance *is* futile. Only a fool tries to insist that this or that event *must* occur though he has no power to cause the event in question. Devote your energies to the proper governance of *your own* mind and *your own* behavior, and learn to accept and embrace all external events as gifts from God or Fate. Remember that you did not *have* to be here at all. The world would have gotten on just fine without you. Here you are, though, and you have the opportunity to live a human life full of wonder, complexity, and adventure—if you just choose to see the events of your life as opportunities rather than calamities. If you wish to be wise and to live in accordance with nature, then you have no business complaining about how nature unfolds and takes you along in confluence with it. The flow of things *will* take you where you are going. Resenting this is both pointless and petulant.

52-c. And this third:

"O Crito, if it thus pleases the gods, thus let it be. Anytus and Melitus may kill me indeed, but hurt me they cannot."
– Plato's Crito and Apology

At his trial, Socrates declared that his accusers might convince the jury to use its lawful power to sentence him to be executed, or that he might be deprived of property or freedom, but also that neither his accusers, nor the jury had the power to *hurt* him. To those who are unfamiliar with the Socratic and Stoic conception of "harm," this may seem an odd, perhaps even paradoxical, claim. If you understand what Socrates and the Stoics taught about the nature of genuine *harm*, however, as opposed to the misguided conception of the masses, this assertion is not difficult to grasp. Your body, your property, and your reputation, are "yours" only in the sense that you have the opportunity to try to take care of them as best you can for a short while. You get to manage these things for a lifetime, in a way that you do not manage those things that belong to your neighbor. In much the same way that you might refer to "your" hotel room, you should recognize that your body, for example, is only "yours" to maintain until death reclaims it and returns it to the dispensation of the natural world. *Everyone* dies. Whether you die from disease, accident, murder, or execution should be of no great concern to you. You ought to be concerned only with those conditions that can be determined by your faculty of deliberation and choice, and only with making choices in accordance with reason, which is unique to human beings among all the other species to be found in the world (as far as we know). Living in accordance with nature is, therefore, living in accordance with *reason*. As long as you deploy reason to help you identify virtue, and as long as you behave in virtuous fashion, no one can do anything to harm or hinder your will and your moral purpose. Even *death* cannot harm the wise. Make yourself into the kind of person that need not fear death. Make yourself fearless altogether. In other words, make yourself virtuous. That is all.

References

The *Enchiridion* (Handbook) of Epictetus: http://classics.mit.edu/Epictetus/epicench.html. Translated by Elizabeth Carter.

BOOKS

SPIRITUALITY

O is a symbol of the world, of oneness and unity; this eye represents knowledge and insight. We publish titles on general spirituality and living a spiritual life. We aim to inform and help you on your own journey in this life.
If you have enjoyed this book, why not tell other readers by posting a review on your preferred book site?
Recent bestsellers from O-Books are:

Heart of Tantric Sex
Diana Richardson
Revealing Eastern secrets of deep love and intimacy to Western couples.
Paperback: 978-1-90381-637-0 ebook: 978-1-84694-637-0

Crystal Prescriptions
The A-Z guide to over 1,200 symptoms and their healing crystals
Judy Hall
The first in the popular series of eight books, this handy little guide is packed as tight as a pill-bottle with crystal remedies for ailments.
Paperback: 978-1-90504-740-6 ebook: 978-1-84694-629-5

Take Me To Truth
Undoing the Ego
Nouk Sanchez, Tomas Vieira
The best-selling step-by-step book on shedding the Ego, using the
teachings of *A Course In Miracles*.
Paperback: 978-1-84694-050-7 ebook: 978-1-84694-654-7

The 7 Myths about Love...Actually!
The Journey from your HEAD to the HEART of your SOUL
Mike George
Smashes all the myths about LOVE.
Paperback: 978-1-84694-288-4 ebook: 978-1-84694-682-0

The Holy Spirit's Interpretation of the New Testament
A Course in Understanding and Acceptance
Regina Dawn Akers
Following on from the strength of *A Course In Miracles*, NTI
teaches us how to experience the love and oneness of God.
Paperback: 978-1-84694-085-9 ebook: 978-1-78099-083-5

The Message of A Course In Miracles
A translation of the Text in plain language
Elizabeth A. Cronkhite
A translation of *A Course in Miracles* into plain, everyday
language for anyone seeking inner peace. The companion
volume, *Practicing A Course In Miracles*, offers practical lessons
and mentoring.
Paperback: 978-1-84694-319-5 ebook: 978-1-84694-642-4

Your Simple Path
Find Happiness in every step
Ian Tucker
A guide to helping us reconnect with what is really important in our lives.
Paperback: 978-1-78279-349-6 ebook: 978-1-78279-348-9

365 Days of Wisdom
Daily Messages To Inspire You Through The Year
Dadi Janki
Daily messages which cool the mind, warm the heart and guide you along your journey.
Paperback: 978-1-84694-863-3 ebook: 978-1-84694-864-0

Body of Wisdom
Women's Spiritual Power and How it Serves
Hilary Hart
Bringing together the dreams and experiences of women across the world with today's most visionary spiritual teachers.
Paperback: 978-1-78099-696-7 ebook: 978-1-78099-695-0

Dying to Be Free
From Enforced Secrecy to Near Death to True Transformation
Hannah Robinson
After an unexpected accident and near-death experience, Hannah Robinson found herself radically transforming her life, while a remarkable new insight altered her relationship with her father, a practising Catholic priest.
Paperback: 978-1-78535-254-6 ebook: 978-1-78535-255-3

The Ecology of the Soul
A Manual of Peace, Power and Personal Growth for Real People
in the Real World
Aidan Walker
Balance your own inner Ecology of the Soul to regain your
natural state of peace, power and wellbeing.
Paperback: 978-1-78279-850-7 ebook: 978-1-78279-849-1

Not I, Not other than I
The Life and Teachings of Russel Williams
Steve Taylor, Russel Williams
The miraculous life and inspiring teachings of one of the World's
greatest living Sages.
Paperback: 978-1-78279-729-6 ebook: 978-1-78279-728-9

On the Other Side of Love
A woman's unconventional journey towards wisdom
Muriel Maufroy
When life has lost all meaning, what do you do?
Paperback: 978-1-78535-281-2 ebook: 978-1-78535-282-9

Practicing A Course In Miracles
A translation of the Workbook in plain language, with mentor's
notes
Elizabeth A. Cronkhite
The practical second and third volumes of The Plain-Language
A Course In Miracles.
Paperback: 978-1-84694-403-1 ebook: 978-1-78099-072-9

Quantum Bliss
The Quantum Mechanics of Happiness, Abundance, and Health
George S. Mentz
Quantum Bliss is the breakthrough summary of success and
spirituality secrets that customers have been waiting for.
Paperback: 978-1-78535-203-4 ebook: 978-1-78535-204-1

The Upside Down Mountain
Mags MacKean
A must-read for anyone weary of chasing success and happiness
– one woman's inspirational journey swapping the uphill slog for
the downhill slope.
Paperback: 978-1-78535-171-6 ebook: 978-1-78535-172-3

Your Personal Tuning Fork
The Endocrine System
Deborah Bates
Discover your body's health secret, the endocrine system, and
'twang' your way to sustainable health!
Paperback: 978-1-84694-503-8 ebook: 978-1-78099-697-4

Readers of ebooks can buy or view any of these bestsellers by
clicking on the live link in the title. Most titles are published
in paperback and as an ebook. Paperbacks are available in
traditional bookshops. Both print and ebook formats are
available online.

Find more titles and sign up to our readers' newsletter at
http://www.johnhuntpublishing.com/mind-body-spirit

Follow us on Facebook at https://www.facebook.com/OBooks/
and Twitter at https://twitter.com/obooks